Me and My Web Shadow

How to Manage Your Reputation Online

Antony Mayfield

A & C Black • London

First published in Great Britain 2010

A & C Black Publishers Ltd
36 Soho Square, London W1D 3QY
www.acblack.com

Copyright © Antony Mayfield, 2010

A CIP record for this book is available from the British Library.

ISBN: 9–781–4081–1908–2

This book is produced using paper that is made from wood grown in
managed, sustainable forests. It is natural, renewable and recyclable.
The logging and manufacturing processes conform to the environmental
regulations of the country of origin.

Design by Fiona Pike, Pike Design, Winchester
Typeset by Saxon Graphics, Derby
Printed in Spain by GraphyCems

Contents

Dedication

For Sarah, Luther & Scarlett-Lily

Web Shadow: **1.** What someone finds when they look for you on the web. **2.** The combination of an individual's online *owned* presence (social network profiles, blogs, personal websites) and their *earned* presence: what others say about them for instance on company websites, blogs, Twitter and wikis. (*Etymology: derives from Jeff Jarvis's term "Google shadow", describing the search results for an individual.*)

Tag: #webshadows

introduction

'Want to see something juicy?'

That was the greeting from Spokeo, a web search engine that finds photos and information about people from 48 social networks. I'd stumbled across it looking for ways people could check out what I was calling their web shadow – the traces of themselves that they or anyone else could find on the web.

What a question.

I was checking my identity online and those of some friends a little less web-obsessed than myself. Entering my email into Spokeo gave me more than that, though – a lot more. Within moments it was delivering hundreds of photos and other information relating to my Gmail contacts; within minutes it had scanned the online lives – the web shadows – of almost 1,000 people that I had corresponded with on Gmail. Friends, colleagues, business contacts, you name it: Spokeo ripped through the web bringing back all sorts of nuggets of information. Most were harmless and entertaining, but there were maybe some that these people didn't intend the world to see.

Who's looking at you?

What happens when someone puts your name into Google or Facebook? If you don't know, you should maybe find out.

Chances are in the past few days or weeks someone has tried to find out about you online. Maybe it was a colleague, maybe it was a prospective employer, a client, a supplier, a bank manager. Maybe it was a spammer or a fraudster or some other individual that might wish you ill.

Our lives increasingly leave echoes, footprints or shadows on the web, whether it's being mentioned in a company press release or a friend putting a picture of us from a weekend barbecue up online. There's no such thing as being unGoogleable, as Bernhard Warner said in an article for *The Times*[1].

---

[1] *How to be unGoogleable*, by Bernhard Warner: *The Times*, May 28 2008 http://technology. timesonline.co.uk/tol/news/tech_and_web/the_web/article4022374.ece

Unless you go 'off the grid' in a really extreme way. And why would you want to go off the grid, anyway? The web is bringing a communications revolution that is unparalleled in the history of our species.

The benefits of understanding the web and the things you can do online at a personal level are also immense. Plus, you get to live through a revolution. Which is nice.

This book is about understanding how the online part of our lives works. How we can manage our online personal presence with a little bit more certainty.

Web shadows

So this book is called *Me and My Web Shadow*. It's adapted from a phrase coined by Jeff Jarvis, one of the most inspiring writers about how the web is changing the world. He called the search results that appear when we put our names into Google our 'Google Shadow'[2].

Your web shadow is the mark you make on the web, the trace of you that people can see there. It's the sum of your presence (social networks profiles, blogs, personal website) and the things that mention you or link to you.

Increasingly, the things we do in our lives end up leaving a trace online. Photos, CVs (or résumé, if you speak US English), company news, blogs, Twitter updates, and all manner of things we and those we know put up on social networks mean that our lives leave an impression on the web.

I work in an industry that for the moment is called 'digital media'. It used to be called 'new media' just a few years ago. Soon it will just be called media. We tend to do that to new things – give them special names that kind of fade away. You can almost hear the words getting shorter and less exotic year by year (cellular telephone, mobile phone, mobile, moby...).

So for now we will talk about our online personal presence, managing our reputation on the web and looking after our web shadows. Soon, sooner perhaps than you think, this will just be how we think about ourselves and our reputation.

---

[2] Jeff Jarvis's *What Would Google Do?* Collins, 2009, is a must-read for anyone interested in the web and its impact on business and society more widely.

Who is this book for?

Me and My Web Shadow is intended as a guide to understanding how to look after your presence on the web: what the web says about you and what it tells people when they come looking for you.

This is a book for anyone who is online but feels like parts of how the web works are running away from them. Also it is for people who want to ensure that they are aware of how the web's growth into so many parts of our lives may affect them, and what they can do to maintain some control over what information is available about them.

You have to write for someone, so I wrote this book for my friends, family and colleagues who need to know more about how the web works and how they fit in as individuals. I have a lot of friends who work with the web, who understand it as well or even better than I do – but most of my friends and family are anxious or unsure about issues such as privacy and personal privacy online.

If you think you're an expert in the web already, there may not be much here for you. But I bet you know some people who might get a lot out of it.

Who am I?

Well, naturally the best way to find out about me would be to Google 'Antony Mayfield'.

Before I worked in 'digital' I worked in public relations and communications, helping brands and organisations understand people who were important to them and how to communicate with them. Actually, I still do, but because I look at websites, online videos, social networks and blogs, I get called something else. Soon it will just be called 'communications'.

I say these things partly by way of establishing my credentials, but also partly to reinforce an important point. The web is quickly becoming un-exotic (although there will always be exotic things to be found on it); it has become a feature of everyday life.

If you were going to be a bit 'self-help manual', a bit 'this book can give your career a digital turbo-charge', a bit 'take your career to 2.0', a bit 'brand-dot-you-dot-zero', you might say that the compelling thing was that this book was about taking the techniques that big brands use to be successful on the web and applying them to yourself.

But that's not the way I see it. Most of what I do is to help brands to understand that the web is a place where they have to operate at a social level, a human level (hence the phrases 'social networks' and 'social media' that are currently in vogue).

How to use this book

I can't help it. I have written for the web for so long that I tend not to think of 60,000 words like this as a document that many people, if any, will sit down and read in a linear fashion, from start to finish. If you do go down that route, I'm sure it will still work, but this book has been written in parts that you will probably dip in and out of as you need them.

- First up, there's a short-ish chapter which should give you everything you need to know to manage your web shadow – the basics, the skinny, the low-down on the basics and the bare minimum you should know. If you're a flighty sort or time-starved, read this and know you can come back to the rest later.
- Second, in Welcome to the Web Age, I set some context around the web; what it means for us and the way that it is changing our world.
- Then, in Managing your web shadow, we get deeper into a recommended approach for getting serious about your online presence.
- Next up, we have what you might think of as the 'Haynes manual' section of the book, dealing with practical use of web tools, social networks like LinkedIn, Facebook, Twitter and how to set up your own website.
- After that cheerful last note, there are some appendices which have links and suggestions for further reading on some of the topics in this book.

This is a personal view rather than an objective one; more of a Mrs Beeton's[3]

---

[3] Not for non-British readers: Mrs Beeton was a Victorian who wrote a book about household management which is mainly remembered for the recipes. Wikipedia has more... **http://en. wikipedia.org/wiki/Mrs_Beeton**

for your personal web, rather than a definitive guide. In truth, I have to be relaxed about this approach – if I'd tried to write a definitive guide I would have gone mad trying. I don't think you can be definitive, absolute, when it comes to something as fast-moving and complex as the web.

This book was out of date six months ago

Sorry to break it to you like that, but it's not as bad as it sounds...

One of the inevitable challenges of writing a book about the web and technology is that things move so fast that some of *Me and My Web Shadow* will be out of date before the presses even start rolling, perhaps even before the publisher clicks 'open' on the Word file. [Note to publisher: go with me on this, I'm making a serious point :-)]

Throughout *Me and My Web Shadow* I have included links to sources and places where you can find more information. There's always a chance that some of these links will be 'broken' by the time this book is printed and you get to read it. In that case, please do visit www.antonymayfield. com/webshadows where there should be links to most things – or you could just try Googling whatever it is you were interested in seeing.

A note about terms: I am guilty of using 'Google' as a synonym for 'search' very often. As 80% of searches in the UK are carried out on Google and it is the company that defined the modern search engine, I'll make no apology for it. Who knows, this 2010 colloquialism could end up looking very dated indeed in a few years' time, but for now, we Google stuff when we want to find it, mostly.

if you read nothing else...

Let's be honest, you are not likely to finish reading this book in one sitting. If you're anything like me with business and reference books you will be lucky to make it halfway through. That's not necessarily a bad thing – usually after a half or even a third of big concept business books you have got the gist. You can dip back into them if you need more detail, but basically you probably have the best of them and it's time to move on.

In fact, this book is part introduction to the brave new world of social networking, part advice piece on how to manage your personal presence on the web and part manual for using various web tools and services.

It practically begs you to dip in and out as you see fit, but hopefully will bear up to – and reward – a straightforward reading from cover to cover.

As a first dip into *Me and My Web Shadow*, try out this section. Then put it down to mull it over, carry on reading, or follow the references to the other chapters that seem interesting.

Why manage your web shadow?

Here are the three most important reasons why you need to think about managing your web shadow:

- **Our lives are moving online:** The web is doubling in size every couple of years, and is drawing in more and more things we do and say: there are going to be more and more traces of you on the web. Becoming a digital hermit will be very hard to do and will cut you off from a great deal of benefits. Best to manage your online presence rather than have it defined solely by what others say.
- **The web is the first place many will look to find out about you:** It is becoming second nature for people to Google one another. Whether vetting potential employees and partners, or simply to know more about colleagues, clients and new acquaintances, people will look online. It is becoming a kind of personal due diligence that you make sure that useful, accurate information about you can be found online.
- **Being findable and connected brings opportunities:** Managing your web shadow, your personal web presence, will often mean using the

web to connect with others and share useful information. This can create great opportunities, personally, culturally, politically or professionally – whatever is important to you. Taking charge of your web shadow will lead to a great level of what we can call 'web literacy'.

The top ten rules for managing your web shadow

When I was thinking about writing a book along the lines of what has become *Me and My Web Shadow*, I was given some unexpected clarity and inspiration from the Chartered Accountants in England and Wales. Their PR agency asked me to help make a video about the 12 Golden Rules for online reputation management. You may still be able to find it online at Vimeo (http://www.vimeo.com/1477988).

Being prescriptive, claiming to be 'definitive', is about the fastest way to trouble there is when it comes to the web. We have to start somewhere, though, so here are the 10 things everyone needs to bear in mind when they are thinking about how to manage their web shadow.

1. Check your Google shadow regularly

No excuses. You need to at least know what Google says about you. The starting point – and the very least you should do if you care about your reputation – is to search for yourself on Google. Google is, for now, the first step on the web journey that most people take.

Unfortunately, the still popular terms for searching for yourself is 'vanity search' or 'ego surfing'. This makes some people feel like they are being immodest, egotistical or navel-gazing by taking a look at what the web says about them. But it is the most basic form of due diligence: managing what people find when they come looking for you.

Now you've checked your Google shadow, you should keep checking it: in two ways. First, set up Google alerts on your name and common misspellings of it. Second: revisit the search results regularly to see what, if anything, has changed about the results that appear (especially on the first half of the first page – most people never look further than the first page of results on a search engine).

2. Be the first/best source of information about yourself

If you are first in Google then you always have the first say about yourself.

Ideally, you should be the number one source of information about yourself on the web.

Why? Because whatever people read about you elsewhere, it may be flattering but may also be out of date, slightly inaccurate, or sometimes damaging to your reputation. Best that the first impressions people get are accurate and yours. If there is erroneous or even negative information about you on the web, it is much less of a worry if people can find out about you from you first, as it were.

This is essentially what we mean by 'managing' your web shadow, or your personal reputation, online. Because the web is open, there is no way that you can control what is said about you (try ringing Google and asking for them to print a retraction) but you can have a big influence on how you are perceived.

As we'll discuss later on, to achieve this you don't have to have your own website (but it definitely helps).

(See *Establishing your web presence* in Part II for more on this.)

3. Understand networks and which ones are important to you

Where are the networks that matter for you, your work and your organisation?

The first thing you should know about the web is that understanding it comes down to seeing it as a network of networks. Everything on the web is connected to everything else. When you see your networks within it, you are looking at clusters of pages that are part of a theme.

The theme could be you. The theme could be your profession, your company, your industry or a million related topics. Pick a handful of keywords, open up a web browser and start exploring. If you focus and spend some time on it, I guarantee you will be amazed by what you find.

Understanding any reputation on the web, whether it's a global brand or a private citizen's, is all about understanding which networks you live in professionally and personally. Where are the blogs, forums and social network groups that relate to your work, family and personal interests? Are you present in them, are you mentioned in them?

Look for places where colleagues and competitors are mentioned. Anyone with a personal website or blog is worth looking more closely at. Who do they link to? What forums and media do they cite?

4. Be present in your networks
Make sure people find you in Facebook, LinkedIn and other places that matter.

Once you understand a little more about your networks, it should be clear where you can establish profiles. You can establish a base, minimum presence – creating a profile without having to commit to updating it all that often.

Most people in, say, the UK (and many other countries) should ensure that they have a presence that is maintained and up to date on LinkedIn and Facebook. At the time of writing, these are the places where the most people have personal and professional presences.

Having a presence makes it easier to understand what is going on that is relevant to you in these networks, and gives you the option to explore possibilities. Think of it as setting up a base.

(See *Establishing your web presence* in Part II.)

5. Be useful
The best way to grow your web shadow is to do useful things to improve your networks.

Search engines and social media are the most important ways that people find things on the web. Both work in basically the same way most of the time when it comes to sending people to places – things that other people find interesting. Attention – the time and energy you spend looking at stuff and the small things you do as a result – is the raw currency of the web. Links and traffic and recommendations make the web go round.

If you want to be found first for yourself, and if you want to go further and grow your reputation online, you need to earn attention. Don't be suckered and try to sucker others with tricks and shortcuts: the best way to earn attention is by graft – by genuinely being useful.

You can be useful in all sorts of ways – joining conversations, giving your point of view, recommending useful content to others – but most useful of all is sharing your knowledge and ideas by publishing them online. Being useful will help you make connections, attract attention and grow, or enrich your network.

6. Draw a line between private and public
There is a line to be drawn and you need to decide to where to draw it.

Living our lives in public on the web is such a new phenomenon for most of us that we don't have any rules, any reference points or any boundaries drawn. (This can manifest itself as that slight feeling of discomfort many have had when their boss 'friends' them on Facebook.)

Practically, we need to understand how privacy works online in technical terms. What can other people see of us through search engines and social networks? What controls can we make use of to manage our privacy?

As a very basic point, since you are very likely to be on Facebook, take a look at your privacy settings. You may not be in the running for the head of MI6 just at the moment, but that doesn't mean that you don't want to keep some information, some photographs, some thoughts to yourself and people you know and trust.

(See *Things you need to know about… Facebook* in Part III for more on privacy settings.)

7. Remember that you are always on the record
There's no such thing as 'off the record', we used to tell our clients who were about to be interviewed by journalists. It applies all the time online.

Even when you delete something on the web, it is likely to exist somewhere else, usually either in the 'cache' of a search engine, or in people's blog-reader, email or Twitter software.

We will discuss being a publisher later on, but something we'll all need to get used to is that we have, in our phones and computers, the ability to publish our thoughts at any moment in front of a billion and a half or so people around the world. So when we are angry, upset, or perceive that a slight has been made against us, it's all too easy – and momentarily may even be satisfying – to vent online.

Four sub-clauses to this golden rule might be:

■ **Normal social rules apply online.** Some say 'don't say anything you wouldn't want to see published in a newspaper'. Even more practical is to remember common rules of politeness: if you wouldn't say something to someone's face, don't say it online. If you *would* say it and they might take offence, be prepared to stand by it and explain yourself.
■ **Pause before you publish.** Pausing before we publish is a habit to get into for the one moment where you are about to broadcast a heartfelt opinion to the world and you suddenly realise you're about to make a fool of yourself. If you're not sure, walk away (or around the block a few times) and come back to re-read what you're about to put out there.
■ **Retraction looks suspicious.** If you are lucky enough to have people paying attention to what you say, subscribing to your blog, following you on Twitter or simply by being a contact on LinkedIn or Facebook, then they will have your content the moment it appears. Pulling that content can ring alarm bells and make people look more closely than they might have otherwise.
■ **Don't drink and blog (or Tweet, or Facebook, or whatever).** Yep, goes without saying. Or at least, it should. Also try not to do it when you're angry – that's just as bad.

8. Get a thicker skin
If you're putting your head above the parapet, don't be surprised if you get the odd disagreement.

The flip-side of not making a fool of yourself online – or at least doing it as little as possible – is learning how to take criticism.

In the early days of my own exploration of online culture and communities, I found this very difficult indeed. English culture, especially in business, is a little over-cautious and leery of upsetting people in public. That means generally not being direct, saying people are wrong to their face, asking for a clear, open debate.

In short, we're a little thin-skinned which, frankly, gets in the way of useful, meaningful discussion. This is especially difficult when it is so hilariously easy to get the wrong end of the stick on the web.

A very clever PR person once told me that the most challenging thing about dealing with high-profile clients with negative stories in the tabloids was that they tended to see a completely different story to the one everyone else was reading. In their minds, they were adding all sorts of details and connotations that weren't there, perhaps out of fear or guilt. Regardless, our perceptions of what people are saying, especially via text on a page or a screen can be very different to what's actually being said by the author.

Remember that it's OK to be wrong, OK to change your mind and also OK to have a different point of view from others. Take disagreement as the useful counter-argument it is: an opportunity to refine or change your point of view.

9. Don't think of the web as another world
The web is all around us – not a strange land that you can choose to visit.

First, perhaps most importantly, we need to get rid of our habit of thinking of the web as another place.

In the 90s, there was a lot of hype about virtual reality (VR), the idea of putting on goggles and stepping into virtual space created by computers. Today, what you are more likely to hear about is augmented reality (AR), where, using camera-phones or special heads-up displays like the ones you would see in a fighter plane, information is overlaid on the real world.

For instance, with the iPhone 3GS you can have an application that lets you point your device's camera at the night sky and on the screen you will see the sky with an overlay of labels telling you what the names of the stars are. In 2008, IBM showed iPhone software for the Wimbledon tennis tournament venue that would give you directions to restaurants and other amenities.

That virtual reality/augmented reality contrast is a useful metaphor for how we think about the web in our lives. Somehow people still often think of the web as separate, something they can opt in and out of.

You probably recall hearing some time ago about the internet and the web described in terms of 'cyberspace'[4]. It seemed like an appropriate analogy at the time. It was intriguing, to see this electronic realm that we were hearing more and more about reflected in science fiction and in the media. People and computers were creating a parallel universe, one which we could kind of step into, as though we were going through the wardrobe into a digital Narnia.

While the cyberspace, VR-like idea was thrilling to some, it was frightening for many others. And in some ways its legacy is that it is too easy for people to almost literally think of the web as another country, a place they don't necessarily need to visit, and one which is full of dark things they would rather not have to have anything to do with.

Rather than C.S. Lewis, maybe we would be better off thinking about the web as being like the magical world of Harry Potter. There are places that are apart from the world, but mostly it exists all around us, simply out of sight to the uninitiated. That leaves a lot of people feeling like Muggles, then. Worse, Muggles who get glimpses of what the digerati are up to. What to do? Ignore them? Rally against them? Or pick up a wand and see what happens?

Let's leave the analogies and come back to earth. An earth that is networked and connected by the web, that is.

The web as we experience it is becoming more like a layer over the world we live in, especially as mobile devices allow us to access it anywhere and make a lot of the information relate very closely to the physical world. Using the web becomes something that enhances the world, augments our ability to make the most of it – not a nether realm that people retreat to darkened rooms with a PC to gain access to.

When I wake up I can know within moments – through my mobile device with web access – what is happening in the world, what my friends and

---

[4] The term was popularised in William Gibson's novel *Neuromancer*.

colleagues are doing and thinking this morning. Going for a run, my exercise information can be registered with my computer and if I choose to share it, posted to my Facebook profile. I know exactly when to leave the house to catch the bus across the road because I can see the live digital timetable on my phone. On the bus I can re-check documents my team have updated ahead of the first meeting of the day with a client. I've not met them before so I Google them and spend some minutes following the links through their online life and know not only what's on their CV, but what they are reading at the moment, that they are training for a triathalon and started a couple of interesting but short-lived photography blogs over the past couple of years. I've never met them before but already they don't feel like a stranger and I'm looking forward to having a conversation with them...

Web shadows are important because so many of the things we say and do end up online. The web is all around us, you might say, all of the time.

part I:
welcome to
the Web Age

1. where the web began

'How are we going to organise all of this information?'

So many thrilling leaps forward – of technology, of art, of *everything* – begin with this simple question.

The web was sparked by problems that came from the vast amounts of information that were being generated by another hugely ambitious technology project, the construction of a machine that would recreate the conditions that existed for nanoseconds at the formation of the universe, the Large Hadron Collider at CERN.

Tim Berners-Lee, a British engineer and computer scientist, asked and then tried to answer this question with a project which created the World Wide Web. A decade or so later, Google expressed its mission as being 'to organise the world's information', effectively by making sense of the trillion or more pages of the web, and by enlarging it by making data, like detailed satellite photography and the contents of the world's libraries, available to anyone.

Now the web is reaching into, including and connecting with all kinds of information about us at an individual level. The question we need to ask ourselves is, How will we organise all of our own information, and how can we manage to some degree the information that is available about us on the web, our web shadows?

We're going to begin here by giving ourselves a context, a basic working understanding of what the web is and how it works. If our lives are going to be present on it, best to know what it is and where it came from.

If you want to get stuck in with understanding and managing your web shadow straight away skip ahead to Part II, but do come back some time – it will help in the long term.

'Rolling amnesia'

If you are ever looking for someone who sees, understands and articulates the profound nature of the revolution that we are living through, Howard Rheingold is your man. Howard coined a term most of us have become familiar with in the past few years, 'virtual community'. He first used it in

1987, about four years before the web was switched on.

In a talk to mobile technologists in Amsterdam in 2009[5], Howard talked about a condition we all seem to suffer from when it comes to technology – 'rolling amnesia':

> 'I don't know whether this is a modern phenomenon, but there's kind of a rolling amnesia about how miraculous things were. You know there was a time when people got lost because they didn't have maps. There was a time when people didn't carry their maps with them with a little line... a little voice that told them where to go.'

Or as Kevin Kelly, the founding executive editor of online magazine, *Wired*, said of the web, 'It's amazing, but we're not amazed.'

Perhaps, from an evolutionary point of view it is kind of understandable that we don't spend years marvelling at the latest gadget or innovation we have been lucky enough to have been given or invented. The success of our species is, in great part, down to its ability to create technology – and then just get on with using it.

So take a pause and remind yourself of the miracle, the wonder, the revolution in progress that we call the web...

A brief history of the web

I didn't have much to do with the web when I started university in 1992. But by the time I left, it was already becoming part of my life...

In 1994 I was studying in Groningen in the Netherlands and I took a one-off class about the Internet. I was fascinated by the idea of the 'net, but without a connection at home or much in the way of technical skills it was all a little daunting.

Email was something I was using a lot to keep in touch with some – mostly American – friends and my early-adopter Dad, and could have a look around at all of the message-boards, but without the hours to put into exploring and learning the culture I did little more than dip in and out.

---

[5] The whole presentation is fascinating. You can watch the video at **http://www.smartmobs. com/2009/06/07/smart-mobs-revisted-at-momo-amsterdam/**

It was just too fiddly with all of the command lines and the like and my biggest use of technology in those days was the cutting edge technology of CD-ROMs, which as a modern historian were a blessing, as trawling through newspaper archives was a whole lot faster with them than the paper or microfiche alternatives.

The Dutch teacher of the class was an enthusiastic junior member of the faculty and showed us how he used messageboards to get ideas for recipes and to catch up on news. It was all very interesting. There were a couple of technologies apart from the messageboards he showed us. One was called Gopher, and you had to enter instructions for it to 'go for' information that you wanted and it would come back with it. It worked quite well.

But not as well as the other technology he showed us. The World Wide Web. To use the World Wide Web you entered addresses into a 'browser' and then pretty quickly you could start navigating around by clicking on the 'hyperlinks'. The web was best for non-technical, arts undergraduates like me. I already understood it after a few minutes.

Sounds obvious now. But then it was just one of a wide selection of ways you could set off into cyber-space into the brave new world of the internet.

Today, 'web' and 'internet' are almost synonymous – that is to say that, to the mild irritation of the technically savvy, people often say web or internet and mean the same thing. Just so you know, let's take a look at a brief timeline of the internet and web's development[6]:

It all started in 1957 with the launch of Sputnik, the first satellite ever launched. The US government was so concerned at this apparent leap forward in technology by the Soviet Union that it formed the Advanced Research Projects Agency (ARPA) to develop new technologies.

Throughout the 1960s, ARPA scientists worked on various concepts around the idea of building a network of computers that would be able to survive a nuclear attack. If all the computers were able to communicate with all the others rather than relying on a few communications hubs, they

---

[6] Take a look at this delightful video for a nice brief version of how the web began: http://bit.ly/qFkI

reasoned, there would be no single point of failure in the system.

Tim Berners-Lee was a British scientist working at the CERN laboratories in Switzerland, a facility that builds infrastructure for nuclear energy research. In 1980, while he was consulting for the organisation, he wrote himself a notebook programme called *Enquire Within Upon Everything* which allowed him to link between individual notes. Nine years later, he was back at CERN and considering the problem of how the organisation would keep track of all the information around its ambitious project to build the Large Hadron Collider, a machine that would famously re-create the conditions around the Big Bang.

In October 1989, he submitted a proposal to his boss Mike Kendall with the modest title *Information Management: A Proposal* in which he sketched out what would become the World Wide Web. Scrawling the words 'vague, but interesting' on the cover, Kendall approved some time and a budget for Berners-Lee to explore the idea.

Work on the first browser and the programming language of the web began in earnest. In 1991, the World Wide Web went live on CERN's servers. Two years later the organisation made a gift to the world by effectively giving the web to everyone, with its directors saying that anyone would be allowed to use the technology without paying a fee to CERN. At this point traffic on the internet was about 0.1 per cent made up by the World Wide Web's use.

The openness of the web was the key to the following two decades of its explosive growth. There was no barrier to people playing with it, tinkering, inventing and innovating. And everything that was created using it could be, and usually was, connected to everything else on the web. Every time a server was brought online running web software, it added more value and possibilities to the network.

In 1994, a company called Mosaic Communications Corporation was founded that quickly changed its name to Netscape. Declaring that 'the web is for everyone' it made available a browser called the Netscape Navigator that quickly became the user-friendly market leader. The following year, Netscape went public and the stock markets fell in love, boosting its share price to heady levels, and arguably sparking what became known as the dot-com bubble.

Thousands of companies were founded in the years leading up to the millennium and a combination of greed, over-confidence and probably the 'fog of revolution' led to a massive over-inflation of the value of companies associated with the internet. In March 2001, the stock markets crashed and there was a bitter backlash in many quarters against the dewy-eyed optimism of the web pioneers.

There was a fairly major exception to the markets' antipathy toward the web, however: Google. Way back in 1996, two Stanford students, Sergey Brin and Larry Page had created a web browser called 'BackRub'. It proved so popular that pretty soon it was causing Stanford University problems with its servers. The next year, they renamed the search engine 'Google' and in 1998 they launched the company proper, working at first out of a rented garage.

A second innovation around a system for bidding for sponsored search results (that run along the top and side of the Google results page) turned a brilliant public service – the best search engine ever created – into a money-making machine. When Google became a public company in 2004, the web was rebounding from the disillusionment of the post-bubble years and there was a new sense of possibility for many in the technology and media communities.

Tim O'Reilly coined the term 'Web 2.0'[7] in 2005 as a way of explaining a new phase in the evolution of the web that he had noticed among the start-ups in Silicon Valley. Web 2.0 was 'an attitude, not a technology', and was about a web where individuals collectively were in control of their data, their content, their services. Values were at the core of this new web, with trust, sharing and participation as key tenets.

And the future of the web?

From here on in there is no roadmap for the web. Futurology, even for the next three to five years, is very hard indeed. The wiser the person thinking about the future of the web, the more likely they are to admit as early as possible that no one really knows what will happen next. As Mark Andreessen,

---

[7] http://oreilly.com/web2/archive/what-is-web-20.html

founder of Netscape (and who has also been involved in companies like Google, Twitter and Ning) says, the web is 'pure software'[8]: there is no end in sight for its continued rapid evolution.

Certainly, mobile web will be a big part of how the web evolves in the coming years. We know that this will mean people using the web even more, creating even more content and accessing services online ever more frequently, simply because it will be easy to. It is also likely that where we are – location or 'geo-location', as the jargon has it – will become something that we can use to get better information and services from the web. Technologies like augmented reality (AR) give us one avenue of possibility for the web's future, but we know better now than to say that anything is a sure bet.

[8] http://video.google.com/videoplay?docid=-4837435862114260403

2. the fog of revolution

Why is it a revolution? And how will it continue?

We are used to looking at revolutions in history.

We also hear the word 'revolution' so often about things happening in the world around us that we are almost immune to the word.

So what does living through a revolution feel like? Well it feels like this: you grow up with three TV channels, 10 newspapers and a handful of radio stations as your sources of information, your windows on the world. It feels like a rate of change where someone who is 40 now, was marvelled at by their parents for being able to work a video recorder or a computer, began their career just as the web was getting started and acquired new technologies in their everyday working lives at a rate of one every couple of years: email, a mobile phone, web browser, search engines that worked, GPS-powered satellite navigation systems and mobile internet, online social networks and information resources beyond their wildest dreams.

Most of these things arrived after they had left formal education. No one trained them, not much anyway. All of these technologies arrived and spread through social networks of friends and colleagues who helped make sense of them.

And actually, though marketing and media futurists have loved lauding and fetishising the 'digital natives', people born in the era of the web, many young people are equally uncertain about how these technologies are transforming the world. Even as they try to make sense of the adult world – challenge enough, for sure – it is breaking itself apart and remaking itself.

Part of us feels like we are already living in the future. Sometimes it's as if we haven't been told anything about the future arriving: it's just there. What are we meant to do with it?

Generals talk about the 'fog of war'. In the midst of battle it is very hard to know what is going on just a short distance away. Decisions are made based on the best information available with a large helping of instinct.

When you are in the middle of a revolution all the noise and confusion of change makes it hard to understand what's going on.

It's an effect that we might think of as the fog of revolution.

Sometimes we latch on to the wrong detail, see patterns where they don't exist. Sometimes we shut down defensively: unable to make sense of what is going on and overloaded by uncertainty we start attacking what is going on. Oversimplify and denigrate it, hope it goes away.

Feeling uneasy?

Maybe living through a revolution means that we experience the cultural and social equivalent of motion sickness. It makes us a little queasy. We would like it to slow down. But it doesn't show any signs of slowing down just yet.

What's the cure? Well in a car we tell people who are car sick to look ahead. Focus on the road ahead and you will feel alright. The advice should be similar for people with revolution rage, revolution sickness: look ahead. Stop focusing on all the dizzying stimuli around us right now and understand where we are going, what the broader sweep of things means.

Science fiction and future-present commentator, Bruce Sterling, talks about the near future as being characterised by a 'dark euphoria', a sense of exhilaration at the pace of change in the world. I live and work with the web more than most, and I think he's right. Even though I get the privilege of watching the edge of the unfurling web revolution every day there are times when it feels desperately uncertain. Too fast, too quick – slow down.

Setting context: the scale and pace of online's growth

Maybe some numbers will help us shake out of our rolling amnesia:

- Google indexes over a trillion web pages today.
- It took radio broadcasters 38 years to reach an audience of 50 million, television 13 years, and the Internet just four.
- In 1998, it was estimated that there were 143 million web users. In 2001, there were 700 million[9]. In 2010, we are well on course for 2 billion

---

[9] UN Cyberschoolbus Report – http://www.un.org/cyberschoolbus/briefing/technology/tech.pdf

people having access to the internet[10].

■ I'm guessing that by the time this book is published, there may be about half a billion users of the Facebook social networking service. It's a total guess, because Facebook continues to surprise us with its growth – it reached the landmark of 250 million users in August 2009 and at the time of writing, it is passing 300 million[11].

■ Currently, about 10 per cent of time spent on the web is spent on social networking activity[12].

■ In the UK, 38 per cent of web users said that they had met someone online that they didn't know before.

Citizens of the networks

Gigi Tagliapietra, President of the Italian Association for Information Security (CLUSIT), is a brilliant conversationalist in his native Italian or English. He says that the massive challenge of web security could never be met by the great anti-virus software companies – who have grown into multi-billion dollar concerns as the web has expanded – alone. Nor can it be met by governments and industry-wide action by Internet Service Providers (ISPs) and computer manufacturers. It turns out we all have a role to play in keeping ourselves safe and making the web a better place.

Gigi described life where he lived in Italy in the winter: every winter, the snows come and block the roads; everyone who wakes up on a snowy morning knows that the first thing they have to do is get their shovel and clear out their own driveway, path and bit of the road.

'If we waited for the local council to come and do it for us, we would all be stuck. The town would stop.'

Everyone relies on one another to do their duty and keep their bit of the town snow-free and working.

---

[10] In late 2009, at the time of writing there were about 1.66 billion connected to the web according to http://www.internetworldstats.com/stats.htm

[11] Facebook reported that it had 250 million users in August 2009.

[12] Nielsen, Global Faces and Networked Places report. http://blog.nielsen.com/nielsenwire/wp-content/uploads/2009/03/nielsen_globalfaces_mar09.pdf

It is the same with internet security, Gigi told me. Everyone needs to keep their parts of it – their websites, their computers, their presence – secure and in order. Where someone is slack, where they don't keep their machines secure, their passwords secret, they leave opportunities for criminals and saboteurs. That affects the wider web: all of us.

We are all citizens of the networks, of the web. We need to look after our part of it, our web shadow and our machines. Not just to keep them virus-free and secure so they cannot be used by hackers to commit crimes and attack political rivals. We need to develop our literacy and understanding of the networks, and take part in the evolution of the web. If we are taking part positively, with awareness of how it works, we are helping to build the future of the web.

The network is us. How this all turns out will in a large part depend upon the collective actions, the clicks and searches and messages of each one of the billions of us online.

If we end up in a nightmarish dystopia because of the web, it will be because we have sleep-walked into that situation, not because we never had a choice. As we become aware of the web, the opportunities, the possibilities, we will need to come to terms with our responsibilities as well.

We all need to keep our driveways clear of snow and trust that all of our neighbours will too.

3. our personal webs

With the web as something we all own (thanks, CERN) and all contribute to, whether by uploading photographs, writing content or just using search engines (Google gets smarter with every search and click you make), we can start to understand the web as the first medium that is truly ours. On the web you are never really a passive consumer, since everything you do creates data, leaves a trace.

So let's think about the nature of our own personal web, the experiences we create for ourselves and the information and communications we create for others.

The social web

We will talk about social media, very much a buzzword in danger of being worn out at the moment, later on. Even before Facebook came into the lives of 250 million of us, the web was social. The web is social; it was from day one.

Barry Wellman, a professor of sociology from Toronto, said the following in 2001:

> 'Computer networks are inherently social networks, linking people, organizations, and knowledge. They are social institutions that should not be studied in isolation but as integrated into everyday lives... The Internet increases people's social capital, increasing contact with friends and relatives who live nearby and far away. New tools must be developed to help people navigate and find knowledge in complex, fragmented, networked societies.'[13]

He is absolutely right, of course.

Let's slay a whimpering myth right here: using the web is anti-social. People who are 'hyper-connected'[14], using multiple online communications tools are more social both online and in the rest of their waking lives, and

[13] Wellman, Barry. 'Computer Networks as Social Networks', *Science*, September, 2001
http://www.sciencemag.org/cgi/content/abstract/293/5537/2031
[14] http://en.wikipedia.org/wiki/Hyperconnectivity

are far less likely to feel lonely, according to research by the Oxford Internet Institute[15].

Tim Berners-Lee's original proposal for the web looked not at just connecting web pages, but everything, including people, to one another.

Suppose each node [points in the network] is like a small note, summary article, or comment. I'm not overly concerned here with whether it has text or graphics or both. Ideally, it represents or describes one particular person or object. Examples of nodes can be:

■ people
■ software modules
■ groups of people
■ projects
■ concepts
■ documents
■ types of hardware
■ specific hardware objects[16]

A public place

The web rewards openness. As it has grown and the 'Wild West' feel has dissipated, the social web has brought people online.

It is far more valuable to other people to know who you are if they are reading what you say. Take review websites like Tripadvisor. A challenge for them is transparency – people want to be able to trust the reviews of the hotels that they are researching. If all the names on the list are anonymous, it is hard to decide whether to believe their objectivity – whether they are the owner trying to leave positive reviews to entice people, or rivals leaving negative reviews.

So the web is a public place, where sometimes it is valuable to reveal information about ourselves. It is also a place where we need to exercise

---

[15] William H. Dutton, Ellen J. Helsper and Monica M. Gerber. *The Internet in Britain*, p.44. Oxford Internet Institute, 2009 **http://www.oii.ox.ac.uk/research/oxis/OxIS2009_Report.pdf**

[16] Berners-Lee, Tim. *Information Management: A Proposal*. 1989

caution in what we say or do, as we don't know who is watching, and everything we do leaves a trace, casts our web shadow behind us as we travel.

Superabundance

One of the greatest challenges for us as we explore the web is that there is so much of it. Google tells us that 20 hours of video are uploaded to YouTube every minute, and the web itself is doubling in size every two years. How do we cope with that? How do we find what we need within all of that? How do we make sure that we are found (when we want to be)?

Web tools: Find out how they work, then find out how to put them to work for you.

- *'Sorry, must take this call.'*
- *'I'm just back from holiday and have 2,300 emails to go through.'*
- *'I've got back-to-backs all day in my diary – it's impossible to actually get any work done.'*

We have a terrible habit of pretending that our machines control our lives. It's a bit silly, because the machines don't really care what we do.

In *Me and My Web Shadow* you will read about all manner of web tools and social networking that can do all sorts of marvellous things. Managing our web shadows should be a way of enhancing our reputations and our lives, rather than adding a whole new dimension of responsibility and a new list of tasks to deal with.

The way to stay the master of the technology is to take responsibility for being in charge of the tools you use. It is your choice if you want to check your BlackBerry® every five minutes, or update your Facebook status equally as often. Sometimes a mild obsession can be helpful while you become literate in a new medium, but then you need to be able to make it work in terms which fit in with whatever you want to do with your life.

4. making sense of the web

The value of networks

Let's get the basics out of the way and have done with it. If you are not a mathematician, sociologist or search engine specialist, you will be delighted to hear that when it comes to networks I am an enthusiastic amateur rather than any kind of expert – so we will be brief.

Networks are composed of nodes which represent whatever the network is made up of: telephones, people or pages on the web. These nodes are attached to one another by connections, which represent telephone lines, relationships or hyperlinks on a web page, depending on what the network is.

In a network the value of the network doubles when just one node is added[17].

If you are the only person in the world with a telephone you have a very expensive paperweight. You would have trouble persuading people of your sanity never mind actually finding any use for the thing. If you give your friend who lives a mile away a telephone you have a very efficient way of having conversations with them and organising visits to the pub at short notice. Once lots of your friends start getting phones, there are all sorts of new uses for it. When shops and businesses start installing them too, well you're away. Every time a new node, a new telephone, is added, it makes the telephone network more useful.

Every time someone connects to the web for the first time, its value increases (doubles?), the possibilities of the network to expand exponentially.

Think about the web again: 1.5 billion people and trillions of pages of information, the equivalent of the entire contents of the Library of Congress travelling around once every minute. Imagine the value in such a thing.

Some of that value comes from your being connected to it. Every time

---

[17] For more on networks see the recommended reading on www.antonymayfield.com/webshadows

you use a search engine you make the network just a little smarter, every time you link to something in Facebook or LinkedIn – yes even the video of an Eddie Izzard sketch set to animated LEGO – you change the network, you add a little to its efficiency.

Mind boggling yet? Good. Let's continue...

My son comes into my study just as I am about to write this. Five years old, he wants to know what I'm doing.

'Work.'

'What work, Daddy?'

'Writing about search engines.'

'What are they?'

So I tell him this story...

When I was 10 or 11, I read The Hitchhiker's Guide to the Galaxy. *All of my friends loved the story. Its title refers to an amazing book, an e-book in fact, a device called the* Hitchhiker's Guide to the Galaxy *that comes with the words 'Don't Panic' in big friendly letters on the front and a database inside it that can tell you just about everything about anything they come across on their adventures.*

I wished I had that book so much. Or at least the Earth-bound equivalent. Looking at the first home computers that we were all beginning to get in our houses (ZX Spectrums, Commodore 64s and the like), it seemed like an impossible dream.

But now I have a machine that can do that and I show him my mobile phone. I open the browser and click on the Google search box.

'Ask any question you want.'

'Animals. Um... About animals.'

'How far can a lion roar?'

'You mean "How far away can you hear a lion's roar?"'

'Yes...'

So I type it. And a second later this what I see...

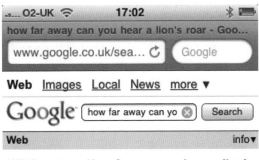

WikiAnswers is the top result to the question and tells us simply 'Two miles'. He's impressed.

'How does it know?'

'People have shared the answer on the website.'

'There must be a lot of scientists who write that. Why do they do it?'

'The scientists share what they know with everyone else and we share what we know on the web too. That way if they want to know something we know about they can find it too.'

He seems satisfied...

A network of networks

Imagine for a moment that we could see the web. What would we see?

Well, if we approached it from a long way off, we would see a cloud of light. If we watched for long enough, we would notice that the cloud was moving, and also moving outward at the edges – growing. Getting closer we would notice points of light within the cloud.

Now let's shake that colossus of a network out of our heads. Now, imagine your web, your web shadow, all the pages that relate to your name.

Let's start with your Facebook page. What is it connected to? First of all, a lot of other Facebook pages – your friends and family. Say you have 40 or so friends, and they all have 40 or so friends. Some of them will be the same people, connect together in a kind of cluster, but most people will have at least a few contacts outside of this, connecting their family cluster, their friends cluster, or their mountain biking cluster of friend pages out to other network clusters.

You can see some of these complex networks and the relationships between them if you use Facebook tools like Circle of Friends[18] or look at the incredible Touchgraph[19] application which will group networks by theme.

Facebook is not the whole web, though. Your page and those of your friends will have links on them to web pages outside of Facebook. To YouTube, to news sites, TV shows' web pages, music websites and other things you have all found interesting enough to share. Some of those pages will be moderately popular – in that other people have linked to them from Facebook and their blogs. Many will have hundreds if not thousands of links to them from other pages – people, search engines and other websites will all be linking to them.

Very quickly our imaginary map of our personal web becomes impossible to hold in our minds. It is simply too complex and we have only stepped one link or so away from our own web page. Even if we tried to draw it out it would get very messy indeed.

---

[18] http://www.facebook.com/applications/Circle_of_Friends/2270425051 (Link only works if you have a Facebook account.)

[19] http://www.touchgraph.com/navigator.html

Whether we look at the web as a mind boggling whole, or from a very local level, it is all about networks from a technical point of view. Thing is, it is also very much about networks from a human point of view.

Search engines and social media: making sense of the web

The good news is that we do not need to hold the web's intense complexity in our minds. Unless you work at a technical level with the web it is unlikely you will ever need to think about it much at all.

As the web has grown in complexity and scale, two complementary approaches to managing our experience of the web have emerged: search engines and social media.

Search engines are a modern miracle, one of the coalitions of miracles that make up the web, along with social media – the collaborative, participatory technologies that allow people to communicate and collaborate.

Search engines: an introduction

Remember your first Google?

Where were you the first time you saw Google? Or the first time you used it? It may be my inner geek and the fact that I work with digital media that means I remember this, but I recall it very clearly indeed. It was in 1998 or 1999, when the web was much, much smaller than today and I was working in a technology marketing firm called Text 100. We had – for that time – a very fast web connection but searching the internet was still a slow process, using services which most people have forgotten as the companies have faded from the web limelight: Alta Vista, MetaCrawler, Lycos. Results took a while to come back and were often filled with spam – sites that were tricking the search engines into pointing users towards their scam sites, e.g. gambling and the rest of the usual suspects.

One of my colleagues, Jörn Sanda, beckoned me over to his desk. There on his monitor was the plain white Google front page. Compared with cluttered, clunky portal front pages of the day it looked like nothing else.

It was a search engine, he explained – not something that filled me with anticipation. I had about 10 search engines I would cycle through while doing research in the hope that one would pull me up some useful results. The last thing I needed was one more to add to the list.

Then he typed a query into the search box and pressed the 'Google Search' button. The results came back in less than a second – and it told us exactly how fast too.

'It's good too,' said Jorn.

I could see what he meant – there wasn't much spam and the results looked exactly what you needed. Instantly I was converted to Google and have been using it almost every day for the past 10 years. Every now and again I will use another one, but mainly out of professional interest.

Google's story has been told many times before, and in more depth than we have time or scope for. For a history of the technology of search take a look at John Battelle's *The Search* and for an inspiring analysis of the implications of Google's approach to the web and to business, take a look at *What Would Google Do?* by Jeff Jarvis.

How search engines work

While we are thinking about search engines and managing our web shadows it is worth explaining how Google works on the most basic of levels.

When Google launched it was instantly better than everything else on the market because of one simple insight: its founders – Larry Page and Sergey Brin – understood that the web was a network, not an information superhighway, not the greatest library ever made.

Yahoo!, the leader of the pack until that moment, had organised itself as a directory, a guide to the web. Editors picked which sites were most useful and categorised them. This approach was doomed because a directory was the wrong analogy. The network was growing too fast for even a large team of people to categorise and file everything as it was created.

Other search engines were using more of a computer-based approach, in that they were trying to get machines to read the pages as they were created and to index them. It was the library analogy again, and it didn't quite work. People don't all think of things in the same way when it comes to categories; they want the same pieces of information for different reasons.

The breakthrough that the Google creators made was called PageRank. It was (and is) a super-efficient way of ranking the importance of pages on a given topic or keyword, based on the links to it.

PageRank borrowed the way that academics judge which of them are the authorities among their peers. They do this by looking at the published works of a given individual and seeing how many times that work is referenced in the published works of other academics. If someone has the most citations for their paper on the print revolution in 15th century Europe, they must be highly regarded by their peers and useful enough to want to reference in their own papers.

PageRank looked at the number of links to a web page, but it also looked at the authority of those pages. So a link from a website with a great deal of authority, say the BBC's website, was a stronger indicator of quality – from the search engine's point of view – than a link from a small company's website.

Twin dark arts? SEO and PR

In 2006, I left the public relations sector after a decade, and joined a search engine optimisation (SEO) firm called Spannerworks. Some of my colleagues in PR (many, in fact), thought I was brave at best, but probably a little misguided.

Now public relations, ironically, has its own image problem as an industry. Thanks to abusers of it as a communications discipline, and our love of a good pantomime villain, the best known PR people tended to be thought of as pretty dodgy: spin doctor bullies squeezing the life and the meaning out of government; sleazy scandal merchants and fixers or Ab Fab featherheads. Most of all, it was – and is – regarded as a dark art.

So you can imagine how delighted I was a week or so before I joined Spannerworks to read an article about SEO in *The Economist* describing that as a dark art too. 'Out of the frying pan...', I thought.

Search engine optimisation (SEO) was a relatively new discipline in marketing which was gaining importance in the digital sector as search engines became ever more important in the way that people used the web. SEO is all about making 'organic' or 'natural' websites appear – or rank – higher in search engine results.

It turns out that PR and SEO were more closely related than I had guessed. As I began to learn the (very) basic elements of how search engines worked I saw that SEO was basically about reputation, just as PR had been. There was one crucial difference: in the world of corporate affairs and brand PR, reputation was an intangible, an unseen, unknown quantity that you could not quantify, but that you had to intuit (guess). With search engines it was the opposite: they had a magic sum (the Google algorithm) that could work out what the reputation of any given page on the web was by looking at what the other pages around it said about it.

Clive Thompson, who writes about the web and digital culture for the *New York Times*, said it best: 'Google is not a search engine, Google is a reputation management system'[20].

---

[20] Thompson, Clive. 'The See-Through CEO', *WIRED* magazine. March, 2007

In fact 'reputation and relevance engine' would be the most accurate description, these two things being the most important qualifications of a web page's importance as Google engineers see things[21].

---

[21] This presentation from Matt Cutts of Google is a great – though technical in places – summary of how Google works… http://searchengineland.com/googles-matt-cutts-video-presentation-on-seo-24234_

part II:
managing
your web
shadow

1. why manage your web shadow?

This web thing isn't going away

Without wanting to sound doom laden, the web is not going to go away. It is still growing and there is no end in sight. As it expands it touches, connects and draws in more of our lives. We need to take control of that.

There are two reasons why each of us needs to take charge, insomuch as we can, of what our web shadow is – especially as it appears to others. First, we can look positively at the opportunities that living with the web brings. Second we can consider some of the challenges, the potential threats that the web's openness and access to our personal lives and information brings to bear on us and our friends and families.

Opportunity unbounded

Shaking out the rolling amnesia from our heads once again, the web presents us with incredible opportunity in every aspect of our lives. We have access to more knowledge, inspiration, entertainment, conversations, business ideas and new thinking than any humans that lived before us.

Taking it down to a more day-to-day level, we can use the web to have more of everything: more friendships unbroken, more understanding of what our career options are, more people we can meet who share our interests.

Synchronicity engines

In his 2004 blog post, *A theory of synchronicity for the web*[22], Richard McManus talks about the way that coincidence increases as a result of being open and exploring new ideas on the web:

> '...synchronicity means to go outside the blog world and explore other worlds. The greater your exposure to different ideas, the more likely you are to formulate new ideas.'

---

[22] ReadWriteWeb: http://www.readwriteweb.com/archives/a_theory_of_syn.php

Another blogger, Flemming Funch said:

> 'We could use a synchronicity engine, really. Some tools that increase synchronicity.'

To my mind, the web is a synchronicity engine, in that it greatly increases the incidence of (mostly) pleasant coincidences.

What I mean, in simple terms, is that the moment that someone starts looking for you on the web they should be able to find you if you have managed your web shadow well. The moment they start looking for someone with your skills or knowledge they may find you, and are increasingly likely to do so if you have a good web shadow. The better your web shadow has been developed, the more likely your name and your links will show up in search engines and social media at precisely the moment it would be fortunate for you to come to their attention.

Web shadows as insurance

You never know when you might need a good web shadow, not just to create opportunity but to ward off misunderstanding and malice. Managing your web shadow means you are listening to what is said about you, so if misinformation or negative attacks on your good name appear on the web, you will know quickly and be able to take action.

A well managed web shadow also means that people who want to know about you will find your information before anyone else's. If you are going to be researched by someone else and not everything about you on the web is in your control, it is simply best if you have the first word.

Be the first and best source of information about yourself on the web

If you've read Part I, you will understand the web becoming an extension of how we think and perceive; not a replacement for thinking or asking questions or being social, but a way of doing those things faster, bigger, better. The web, and our access to it via search engines and social networks, is like our personal information superpower.

Looking after your web shadow, paying attention to your online personal presence and the things around you online is about caring for your reputation.

The simplest way to do all of these things is to ensure that when people come looking for you online, your information – what *you* want to say about you – is the first thing that they find.

Careers and business

When we think about our online web presence and how it affects our lives, work is the first thing for many of us that comes to mind. For those of us who want to put in the minimum effort to managing their web shadow, looking after the career or business side of things should be the priority (at least if people from other spheres of our lives come looking for us they will see some professional information, which is unlikely to be a bad thing).

The always-on CV

A useful, central metaphor for our web shadow might be a 24/7 CV that is always available to anyone who wants to know more about us. A personal website or LinkedIn profile (see *Things you need to know about… LinkedIn*, Part III) will do this job for us.

A professional profile is already a standard requirement in many industries. Statistics from recent reports in the UK and US suggest that many or most employers will use social networks like LinkedIn and Facebook, as well as dig deeper for information, using Google to:

- identify candidates for jobs;
- short-list applicants;
- background check potential employees.

While no one is going to hire someone without having looked them in the eye and contacted a few references, in some instances having a healthy web shadow or not is what defines whether individuals are considered at all.

Of course this will be the case when you are looking for people who work in specific areas of online media, such as social media companies, PR or marketing companies, or in digital roles at big companies. But this trend is spreading – a non-existent or shabby web shadow means someone is not really engaged in digital culture.

In larger organisations, it is not uncommon now for people to use the web as well as internal systems to look for information about colleagues when putting together project teams. If your web shadow is incomplete, hard to find or doesn't have all of your skills and accomplishments visible, you may miss out.

Freelancing and consultants

If you are one of the growing number of independent consultants, contractors or freelance professionals in the workforce, a well-maintained web shadow is a sensible extension of your existing reputation and network. Making sure that your skills and experience are findable and well-presented must surely be a basic form of due diligence for your personal business.

Web shadow as employment insurance

If you are in full-time employment, you might also think of investing small amounts of time in your web shadow as a kind of employment insurance. There is a certain sense of security in growing a web shadow presence and a network, as you know that should you need to find a new job, or set yourself up as an independent contractor, you have a base to do that from at a moment's notice.

Privacy

Understanding and managing issues around your privacy and the privacy of those you care about is another reason to take managing your web shadow seriously. In this area, it is a case of not waiting for problems to manifest themselves in our lives but getting in there first and understanding what can be done to take care of our personal privacy.

Online privacy is a complex issue that we all have to grapple with. Developing an understanding of how your web shadow works will give you insights into what you can and can't have an influence on and to manage simple things – like privacy settings on social networks – that can have big implications.

Personal reputation

The definition of reputation we will use here is that it is the sum of what you do and what others say about you.

In managing your web shadow, you can bring together all the things that people say about you, for instance in the form of endorsements on your LinkedIn profile. When people look at who links to your blog, search on your Twitter user name or just plain search for you on Google they will assess your reputation accordingly.

In professions where people work with technology, the web or media, searching for someone and not finding much said about them can raise questions. Haven't they done anything people think is worth talking about? They claim to understand the web, but there's hardly a trace of them on it...

While that is not the case for other industries, it is likely that it will become so, as the web grows and becomes the place where all our trade news journals, conferences and professional activities take place or leave a trace.

'Brand You' v. Being Yourself

For some people, thinking about their reputation, and their online reputation specifically, the idea of personal branding is a powerful one. For others it is a little unsettling as a concept. Perhaps it is a British thing, but there's a sense of trying too hard, being a little too desperate or possibly misleading others. Certainly Americans seem to feel a lot more comfortable with the concept – maybe something to do with the culture of 'can-do' self-confidence that seems to prevail there.

Tom Peters, the US business guru coined the phrase 'Brand You' and explains it in an article for *Fast Company* magazine like this[23]:

> 'You're branded, branded, branded, branded. It's time for me – and you – to take a lesson from the big brands, a lesson that's true for anyone who's interested in what it takes to stand out and prosper in the new world of work. Regardless of age, regardless of position,

---

[23] http://www.fastcompany.com/magazine/10/brandyou.html

regardless of the business we happen to be in, all of us need to understand the importance of branding. We are CEOs of our own companies: Me Inc. To be in business today, our most important job is to be head marketer for the brand called You.'

It is down to you how much you want to think in these terms. Just remember that brands, like reputation, are designed as an intention, but are defined, just like reputation, by what people actually think of them.

Reputation rating

Another metaphor that may be helpful is to think of the web like a wide open credit reference agency for your reputation.

If you are going to apply for a loan or a mortgage, the provider will call a credit reference agency (such as Equifax in the UK) and ask them for a rating. The agency looks at your record as a debtor, how often you've borrowed, how much and if you've ever missed payments and then does some arcane maths to work out if you're good for the loan. The better your record, the more likely it is to recommend that you get the loan. If you come out with a low score, they may still let you have the loan but with a higher interest rate.

We all kind of understand the principles behind our credit rating, and act accordingly. It's an incentive to pay things back on time, and if we are particularly worried or fastidious we can take a look at our records, correct any errors and take courses of action to improve our rating.

Outside of the 'computer says no' routines portrayed by *Little Britain*, where clerks in banks or stores blankly repeat our fiscal fate based on what their database says about us, our reputation rating is a little more complex.

In 'small world' industries, like the law, media or banking, where everyone is only a degree or two separated from everyone else working in it, your reputation is everything. If there is a decision to be made about hiring someone, or partnering, or investing in a venture, a phone call to a friend of a friend is an important part of due diligence, of checking that the person in question can be relied upon.

The web is making all our worlds smaller. A check on LinkedIn can show you that the person you're about to hire once worked with a friend from college. Dropping an email to that friend and a discreet conversation later you can be clear about just how much of a role they played in landing the major account and why exactly they decided to leave the company after just 10 months.

Interestingly, Zopa, an innovative 'social lending company' that helps groups of people lend to individuals, asks people applying for a loan for their eBay seller score if they have one. Again, what other people say about you is hard to fake.

Identity

It may not be long before we start using our web shadows, or part of them, to prove who we are. Think of your web shadow in this context as your portable, digital fingerprint.

Imagine if a website was looking at how it could allow comments on its articles, keep them high quality and avoid spam. One way would be to check the social graph (the network map of their friends on social networks) to prove that they were a human and not a spambot (a computer programme that tries to leave adverts and links in the comment sections on people's blogs). It is hard to fake a set of human friends, and not too hard to spot people who are pretending to be humans. When people are using their own real identities they tend to be a lot more polite too.

Similarly, consumer reviews websites are constantly having to deal with people (illegally in the UK) faking reviews for their own products and services. Services like Facebook Connect, Google Connect and OpenID allow people to sign in to these services, proving who they are, even if they want their review to be anonymous.

Learning and literacy

We talked about digital literacies in the last section, so I won't labour the point here. Suffice to say, that the process of learning to manage your web shadow, and the ongoing management of it will help you to develop skills and literacies that will help in other parts of your working and personal life.

Citizenship

Being alive today means that you are a citizen of the web, almost by default. There are issues around personal freedoms and privacy and ownership of data being debated and discussed in our societies and by our governments that can have profound implications for our lives and the lives of those who come afterwards.

Taking responsibility for your web shadow, for your corner of the web, as it were, will give you an understanding of these issues and let you participate in the public debate around them from an informed standpoint.

On a practical level of real-world citizenship, an understanding of the web as a medium can be an incredibly powerful thing in galvanising communities of support around issues that matter to you, whether that is campaigning for a political party or a local planning decision.

We can be better citizens – re-connect with communities where we live. A Luddite's reaction to the web is to claim that it makes people more isolated, but the reality is that it can de-atomise society faster than anything, bringing people together around issues, whether they be environmental campaigns or organising a street party.

2. exploring your web shadow (and beyond)

Approach

Make a plan

The key to web research of any kind is to have a plan, stay focused and know when to stop digging. You can go on clicking on interesting links forever otherwise.

What you will need is a list of keywords, including:

- your name, and any aliases (profile names on forums, maiden names);
- common misspellings of your name (I'm as often 'Anthony' as 'Antony');
- your trading name, if you are a small company or sole trader.

> Note: You may want to expand this list to include family members' names if you are helping them with this too.
>
> If you have a name that you share with a lot of people, e.g. John Smith, or Claire Brown, then try adding some other words to your name, like where you live, company names, initials etc.

Keep notes, make a map

Be ready to take notes and keep web addresses next to notes too (using Delicious bookmarking with the private check-box ticked could be a good way to do this).

Take note of:

- **Positives:** There could be media coverage or mentions of you that you are not aware of. These may be things to link to or include as part of your profile on social networks or blogs. (You may like to drop a note to thank people who have, for instance, blogged about your work, or leave a comment on their site if the facility is available.)
- **Negatives:** There may be criticism of you, misinformation or embarrassing content. Don't react immediately (especially not in anger).

- **Doppelgangers:** Almost everyone has a double out there when it comes to their name, or at least people who can be mistaken for them. Make sure you are aware of who they are – it will help you develop a strategy for making sure your web shadow is distinct from theirs, and will help you clear up misunderstandings faster.
- **Interesting things:** Make sure you make a note of or bookmark anything that looks interesting, e.g. blogs and forums that mention you in passing and might be interesting to get involved in or read later on.

Google yourself

The chief tool for understanding how the web sees you is Google. In itself it is a powerful search engine and, therefore, specifically designed for exploring the web, for finding things. Google is more important than that, though; it is everyone's front page of the web, where most people start in their attempts to find something out (eight out of 10 searches in the UK are on Google). For everyone, from rock stars and politicians, to first jobber graduates going for an interview, the front page of Google is almost more important than the front page of any newspaper, report or CV.

Sanity, not vanity

So it's not vanity, but plain old, feet-on-the-ground common sense that you need to see what Google says about you when people go looking on the web.

The start is simply putting your own name into the search engine. Let's take a look at the anatomy of a personal search.

- **The Google front page:** The front page of Google is by far the most important on any set of search results – few people will go further than this. The first four or five results are also much more likely to be read than those lower down, so pay close attention to what is showing up here.
- **Logged out:** For a real picture of what most people will see when they search for you, make sure you are logged out of Google (you will be logged in if you are using Gmail, Google Reader or any other Google

services). Log out by using the link in the upper right hand corner of the screen.

- **Unquoted/quoted search term:** You can sometimes see different results if you search for your name inside quotation marks (Google looks for pages with those two words next to each other) and without. Try both, if only because people looking for you may use either.
- **News results:** If you have been mentioned in any press releases from your company or in the media more widely, you may see News results. Sometimes, Google will embed other kinds of results, e.g. video, in search results, if they are available (see 'other services', below).
- **Indented:** Where there are indented results, these are pages on the website listed above it that also reference you. Google is trying to guess which results will be most useful to the person searching when it does this. Perhaps the indented result is a recent addition or got a lot of links.

Refining your searches

You can refine your searches in several ways:

Use different 'search syntax': by adding different words and symbols in the Google search box you can see different kinds of results. Take a look at http://www.google.com/help/cheatsheet.html and Google's help function for more. The following are also particularly useful:

- **OR:** 'your name' OR 'yourname' – brings up results for both;
- **'-':** putting the minus symbol against a second word will strip out results for the second word, e.g. apple pie -mom (useful for stripping a bulk of results to do with someone else's name or a previous company you worked for that creates a lot of 'noise' in the results against your name;
- **'site:':** finds results within a specific website, e.g. yourname site: www.yourcompany.com;
- **'link:':** finds pages that link to a specific page or website, e.g. link: www.yourcompany.com.

Use the advanced search options: Click on the 'Advanced options' link to the right of your search box to refine your search results by excluding or including specific words.

Search options: Clicking on the search options link below your search box on the left of the screen will allow you to filter results by seeing just results from forums, videos, and by time, e.g. the past 24 hours, week or year.

Other services: Along the top of your Google search screen will be the other Google search services. You should check Images, Videos, News, Groups and – you never know – Maps. Be sure to take a look at the other services that are available too – Google is always adding them.

Setting up your Google Alerts

Before you leave Google to continue exploring your web shadow, be sure to set up some Google Alerts, using the keyword sets around your name (you may want to add in some for your company while you are there). To use Google Alerts go to http://www.google.com/alerts and set up alerts to email you once a day on a comprehensive search as a default.

FAQ | Sign in

Google alerts
beta

Welcome to Google Alerts

Google Alerts are email updates of the latest relevant Google results (web, news, etc.) based on your choice of query or topic.

Some handy uses of Google Alerts include:

- monitoring a developing news story
- keeping current on a competitor or industry
- getting the latest on a celebrity or event
- keeping tabs on your favorite sports teams

Create an alert with the form on the right.

You can also **sign in to manage your alerts**

Create a Google Alert

Enter the topic you wish to monitor.

Search terms:	
Type:	Comprehensive ÷
How often:	once a day ÷
Your email:	

Create Alert

Google will not sell or share your email address.

Where else to look

If your search for yourself (as it were) on Google yielded some interesting forums, blogs or social networks that mentioned you, spend some time exploring them further for mentions of you and things that are connected to you (colleagues, companies, competitors, well-known people from your field).

This is then the time to cast your net a little wider, looking at social media sites and using some specialised tools.

Social media sites

Social networks: Not all social networks are visible to search engines, so you will want to go into these and take a look yourself. If you and people in your networks have little to do with most social networks, then you may just want to check Facebook at this stage. You will need to set up a profile with Facebook and other social networks if you don't have one in order to be able to use their search engines properly. Even then you may not be able to see all content, as often privacy settings restrict viewing to members and their connections/friends.

Specialised tools

Twitter Search (http://search.twitter.com): Twitter's always worth checking, even if you aren't on it. Google does index it, but it doesn't seem to pick up everything in alerts.

Socialmention (http://socialmention.com): A great search engine for finding mentions of people, especially if they are active in social media. Select different formats, e.g. blogs, microblogs (chiefly Twitter) and images.

Spezify (http://spezify.com): Not comprehensive but highly visual and surprisingly fun. If you don't get a result at first try combining your search with keywords about where you work or live.

Touchgraph Google visualisation (http://www.touchgraph.com/TGGoogleBrowser.html): We've saved the best until last in this section. Touchgraph is a data visualisation company, but they let people try some of their tools for free, including this one which creates network maps from Google results.

It may not give you any information that you can't get out of a Google search, but it is a lot of fun and lets you see the results of a search as a network, which is closer to the truth of how the web works than a list.

My Touchgraph network shows my blog, my profiles on LinkedIn and SlideShare, iCrossing (where I work) and the blogs of two of my colleagues, Alisa and Dax as the closest things to the centre of my web shadow.

This is really the closest thing you will get to seeing a visualisation of your web shadow, actually your Google shadow, as Jeff Jarvis coined it. It's worth spending some time playing with your Touchgraph by zooming in and out and clicking on nodes to see what they connect you to.

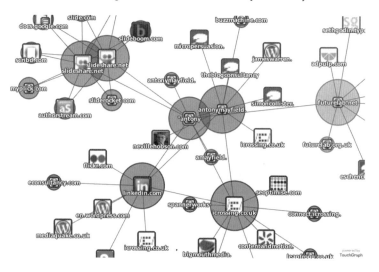

Take a look at *Useful tools for managing your web shadow* in Part III for online tools that will help you speed up your exploration of the online world.

Exploring your wider online world
Find a web savvy colleague or friend

The first question to ask yourself is: do you work with anyone who is blogging or using social networks for work? If you don't, ask around and try to find someone who is. Have a chat with them and ask them where's useful and interesting. Having a good read of their blog and taking a look at any other social media services they link to from there first would be a polite thing to do. If they are using Twitter or a bookmarking service like Delicious, then you're likely to find a wealth of links to useful and interesting stuff.

Trade media
Tools and scores

There are a good few tools on the web that will help you get an idea of what your web shadow looks like.

Take scores with a pinch of salt. They are often about as useful as those magazine 'understand what kind of person you are' quizzes – way too simplistic to apply to your individual circumstances.

Tools are useful, then, but it is much more important to get a feel for how findable you are, and what Google and the rest of the web says about you.

Have a look at the online industry magazines for your sector. Do they have forums? Some trade publishers have developed forums – for instance teachers exchange lesson plans on the TES (*Times Educational Supplement*) website, while on the *Estates Gazette* website, the trade journal for commercial property professionals, the journalists are blogging about (and therefore linking to) all sorts of interesting and useful information and websites.

Inside your work: Take a look inside your organisation. Although many intranets are deserted, desolate places, some organisations have taken some of the most interesting communications ideas from the web and brought them inside their own networks. Finding people who are active on internal social networks, forums, messageboards and blogs can be a great way to connect with colleagues, but you're also likely to find people there who will point you to the best places online for your industry or area of professional interest.

Following the link trails: If you are lucky enough to find some people you know via online media who seem to be interested in the same things you are, it is simply a case of following the link trails. You'll come across some dead ends for sure, but pretty soon you will begin to see where the interesting online places are for your work and other interests. Make sure you 'favourite' the websites you discover along the way, or even 'bookmark' them in a service like Delicious.

Google it: Naturally, the best way to go exploring on the web is to use Google (or the generic search engine of your choice). The most methodical way (and there's really no need to be all that methodical) is to select some keywords associated with your work or personal interests. For instance, if you are a project manager in a civil engineering firm who likes mountain biking you might want to build a list like this (come to think of it you'll probably be thinking of your own much more rigorous method already):

- 'civil engineering' (if you didn't know, putting phrases inside quote marks really helps narrow down searches)
- 'civil engineer'
- 'project management'
- 'PRINCE2' (a widely used project management framework)
- 'project manager'
- 'MTB' (an abbreviation of mountain bike)
- 'mountain biking'

Then start searching with all these terms plus words like 'blogs', 'forums' and 'communities', i.e.: 'civil engineering' forums, 'civil engineering' blogs, 'civil engineering' communities.

Have a look through some of the top results – the front page or two, or more if you keep finding interesting hits. Whatever takes your fancy.

Judging forums by their looks: Don't be fooled by poor design: often, very vibrant and interesting online communities exist in very drably designed websites. Sometimes the inverse is true: a slickly designed corporate-sponsored community can have everything on the surface but no real community means that it will be a sterile, dull place to spend time. Much more important in gauging whether the community is of interest are things like how often people are posting there and what they're talking about. A community with a handful of members that post a couple of times a month is unlikely to be an interesting place to hang out (although I'm sure someone will find an exception to the rule – the web's like that).

3. making a plan for your web shadow

Time to make a plan

OK, stop. Now you have had some fun exploring your online networks, it's time to get serious and make a plan. There is no need to go overboard and start plotting timelines and Gantt charts (if you haven't come across the latter, pray you never do), but it is very helpful to go through the planning process for your web shadow.

If you are an ace project manager or *über*-strategist, maybe you can skim this chapter, but for the rest of us, let's walk through the elements we will need to consider in planning the management of our web shadows.

Assess your situation

Now you have an idea of what your web shadow looks like, write out a frank assessment of it. What's good? What could do with improvement?

If you want to get business-like with it you might want to use some planning methods like SWOT (listing strengths, weaknesses, opportunities and threats). It's actually a quick way of moving through everything you need to consider in managing and growing your web shadow.

Be clear about your objectives

Note down what you would like to achieve by managing your web shadow. We might start with one or all of the following:

- enhance your personal reputation;
- ensure you're findable online when people look for you;
- guard against identity hi-jacking/mistaken identity;
- learn more about how the web works.

Perhaps think about tying in some goals from your personal or working life:

- prepare to go freelance/start a business;

■ get a new job;

■ find/meet other mountain bikers in Sussex to form a riding group.

Personal reputation: being v. 'appearing'

To return to the theme of 'personal brand', you can't re-invent or re-design yourself online in the context of managing your web shadow. This is about making the best of who you really are, not concocting a fantasy super-self that is somehow going to dazzle people into offering jobs, dates, contracts or whatever.

There's plenty written on the subject of personal online reputation management. The subject even has its own acronym (ORM) which is always a worrying precursor that should get your Rheingoldian 'crap detector' antennae twitching, even if it is well meant.

Some of the advice leans more toward 'appearing' to be useful and interesting, rather than actually being interesting. For instance, some advice I came across recommended buying articles or blog posts to publish on your website rather than writing them yourself. This may work if you have really turned yourself into an online brand of sorts, but for most of us it is faking it and that's just not going to go down well with people.

Web-business celeb Guy Kawasaki has ghost-writers help him out with his Twitter page and his blog, but arguably he has reached the point where his name really is a brand and he is simply acting accordingly. He is also open about the processes he uses to connect and cross-promote his various companies and blogs[24].

For most of us, I would say the advice is simple: do it yourself or don't do it at all.

Then again, maybe half-faking it, taking the personal-brand-on-steroids approach is right for you, your business or just plain fits in with the network which you want to be part of. In which case you will probably think that I am just engaging in what Mr Kawasaki calls *bull-shiitake*.

---

[24] Guy Kawasaki's How to change the World blog: How to use Twitter as a Tool, 2nd December 2008 - http://blog.guykawasaki.com/2008/12/how-to-use-twit.html#axzz0R3olknK4

Your approach to your personal reputation, to developing your web shadow, has to be something you feel comfortable with. Someone at some point will tell you that you're doing it wrong, and when that happens you will simply need to work out whether you agree or not.

Action!

If you are working through this book in a linear way, then you won't be ready to complete your plan at this point. That's fine: it should always be a bit of a work-in-progress as you learn more about the web and develop your skills and interests. For now, treat your plan as an outline, but keep it close by (a document saved on your computer desktop, for instance).

Naturally, everyone's plan for developing their web shadow should and will be very different. Things to consider are:

- **Where to establish a presence:** You will need to cover at least Facebook, LinkedIn and be seriously considering Twitter and a personal blog. We'll cover more of this in *Establishing your web presence* later in Part II.
- **How to listen/read:** You have your Google Alerts set up, but be clear about other ways you will be listening not just to what is said about you but to conversations relevant to your work or your goals for your web shadow.
- **Where to join in:** You will need to commit to a community or online group to get the most out of it and learn how it works. At first you may have your hands full with whatever basic presences you start with in LinkedIn, Facebook and your blog or Twitter, but you may have come across communities you want to be involved in while exploring your web shadow. Think about how you will prioritise these.
- **How much to invest:** Since most services on the web are free (beyond things like buying a domain and hosting your own website), the main investment you need to factor into your planning is how much time you can dedicate to the project. How will you fit it all in? Allow a good amount of time in the first few months for establishing your web shadow and learning about new tools, and after that you will just need

regular reviews booked in to your diary. You should also be incorporating activities that enhance your web shadow into your day-to-day working routine.

Starter plan checklists

The following are some starter suggestions for action plans around particular challenges. As you get used to managing your web shadow and become a part of the networks around your work or interests, you will begin to find new ways to be useful and get more out of playing a part in those networks. So, be ready to change your plans often, but try some of these out for starters...

Just the basics

Want to make sure you're not doing yourself a disservice by being invisible or hard to find online? Want to be the first/best source of information about yourself and maybe get a few opportunities come your way? Then you need to have a working, interesting and easy-to-find web presence.

Steps:

1. Establish complete profiles on LinkedIn and Facebook. Connect with all professional contacts on LinkedIn. Ensure privacy/friend groups are set up properly on Facebook (see Part III's guides for more information on Facebook privacy and LinkedIn).
2. Buy your own domain name and post a simple page with links to LinkedIn and some way to get in touch with you.
3. Make people aware of your online presence. If appropriate, add your LinkedIn or other URLs to your email signature.
4. Stake out your profile name in other social networks and professional spaces in case you want to access them or become useful. Also guard against the (mostly unlikely) possibility of identity hijacking – a very dramatic name given to the practice of impersonating other people online.
5. Conduct regular reviews to ensure your information is up to date and achievements are listed etc. Make sure that new contacts are added to LinkedIn.

Growing your presence/network

Really want to give this a go and explore what having an online reputation could do, where your networks might lead you?

You'll want to make sure you have the basics covered (see above) and also...

1. Time, time, time: The most important part of your plan will be agreeing with yourself that you are going to invest time in trying things out, developing your profiles and creating content.
2. Create and connect: Growing your presence and network means earning attention from others. The best way to earn attention in networks is to create new things: industry analysis, inspirational videos, real-world meet-ups, online groups, round-ups of news about your field, whatever you find is something you can do well. Make sure all your presences link properly – use your Google Profile or a similar service to make sure everything ties together and people can find all the different elements of your online presence.
3. Use blogs and Twitter: If you are serious about developing your online reputation you have to at least give blogging and Twitter a good try (see the guides in Part III for details on how to get these set up). Even if you decide they aren't going to work for you in the long-run, you will learn a lot about networks and how the web works from them.
4. Invest in being an active LinkedIn user: For growing your personal network, few places online match the potential of LinkedIn. As well as using it as your live CV and contacts book, make sure you explore the Groups and Answers features of the service. Look at what people in your network are linking to, what they are talking about and which groups they belong to.
5. Read a lot and try new things: Experimenting and exploring will be a big part of developing your web shadow. The web's too big a place for a book like this to cover everything: make sure you are regularly reading the blog of people who are experts in your field, as well as related areas. Following links from their blogs will take you to all sorts of interesting places.

Enhancing your professional reputation
Making the most of a fair reputation in your work, by taking it online.

1. **Establish profiles in professional and social spaces:** Explore postings from top bloggers talking about your area and other online media that report on it. Look at the web shadows of commentators and leading figures to see if you can find interesting groups online. Join them, complete your profile and start listening to see if it is somewhere you should be active.
2. **Begin a blog:** Even if it is just short comments on interesting news articles and snippets of useful information, get your blog going.
3. **Share your work:** If you are writing or presenting about things that can be shared in the public domain make sure you are doing so (see SlideShare in *Useful tools for managing your web shadow* in Part III) and connecting the content to all your different profiles to give people the best chance of seeing it.
4. **Add to conversations:** Where there are interesting comment discussions on blog posts or industry news articles, join in. Follow the links in these to discover other people interested in your area and connect with them: start following them on Twitter and reading their blogs, for example.
5. **Look for real-world meet-ups of online groups:** If you are becoming part of an online community of professionals, keep an eye out for mentions of conferences or meet-up events members are attending. It's great to strengthen an online relationship with the best kind of conversation, a face-to-face one. (If you've never done it before, there's an odd feeling about meeting an online contact and launching straight into discussion without having to go through small talk. You already know each other pretty well, even though you've never met.)

Looking for a job
If you're unexpectedly out of work, re-entering the job market or just looking at your next move. Naturally, I'm going to say make sure you are

doing everything in the previous three sections, but these points will help you go the extra distance you may need to cover to land your dream job...

1. First-class online CV: Where can you make sure there is a copy of your CV available? As well as having a tip-top LinkedIn page, post a copy of a downloadable version on Scribd, Google Docs and SlideShare that is connected to your blog and LinkedIn page (see notes on these in Part III). Make sure you have a web-safe CV – that is, one with just the contact details and personal information that you want to appear on the open web.
2. Hunt down the head hunters: Recruiters use LinkedIn and other networks to find candidates. Make sure that your profiles include keywords relating to your sector or the job you want. And then go looking for them...
3. Ask your network: Like so many things in life, the best advertising is word of mouth when it comes to jobs. Many positions never make it to ads or recruiters – plus many people feel more comfortable hiring based on personal recommendation. If you have a network on LinkedIn, Facebook and elsewhere tell individuals that may be able to help you that you are looking for new opportunities. Make sure that you send a link to LinkedIn and/or your portfolio or CV.
4. Find job boards, groups and feeds: There are plenty of services where jobs are advertised. If you can create a profile make sure you do so and post links to other places you have useful information about yourself and your work.
5. Be open, if you can: If you're already in employment, it's understandable that you may not want to broadcast that you are job hunting to your boss. But the more open you can be about what you are looking for the more likely you are to stumble across the perfect opportunity. It's certainly worth considering updating your Twitter, Facebook and LinkedIn accounts with progress and thoughts on your quest, keeping it as upbeat as you can. If it sounds desperate, you may put people off.

Working for yourself

Depending on the nature of the work, freelance and contractors can get a great deal of benefit from developing their web shadow. Borrow points from the professional reputation plan and use these as you see fit.

1. Look for online marketplaces: Some types of work have online market places that match skilled professionals with work, such as Elance (http://elance.com). Craftspeople, artists and designers are using eBay or dedicated marketplaces like Etsy (http://etsy.com) and Supermarket (http://supermarkethq.com) to sell their products direct and attract commissions. See if there is something similar in your area by searching and asking other professionals. As with LinkedIn and other professional networks, make sure you put effort into completing your profile and, if you are not going to be active, link to places where you visit more often.
2. Dedicated communities: People who work for themselves have lots of online support networks, communities, forums, blogs and even email lists. Look around to find ones which work for you – joining will bring all sorts of benefits in terms of advice, networking and even work.
3. Check how the best people in your field work their online presence: If you find someone who appears to be using the web particularly well, try going through the same process you used to look at your own web shadow with theirs. You're likely to uncover interesting websites and tactics that you can emulate.
4. Showcase your work: Find ways to showcase your work. Even if you don't have a website, use photo websites and SlideShare to create slideshows of projects and experience. Images can be used to bring projects and experience to life – brand logos, buildings, iconic city locations can serve well as illustrations, even if the output of your work is not visually exciting (say accounts, legal opinions or back-end software code). Try writing two- or three-line accounts of projects, and get testimonials approved by satisfied clients that you can include. All of these can be showcased on an About Me page on your blog (yes, you should have one) and on your LinkedIn profile.

Moving on from past problems

Everyone makes mistakes, and everyone moves on. Sometimes, however, things like an arrest, legal problems or insolvency stay with us in our web shadow. If it is the recent past or things like a bankruptcy or court case are being worked through, it may be better to have these matters resolved before you embark on rebuilding your reputation. We discuss more around dealing with negative elements in your web shadow in *Dealing with bad things online* later in Part II.

- **Put your best (web shadow) foot forward:** Perhaps even more so, you need to be the first/best source of information about yourself on the web. If people dig deep enough they will always find things about your past online. Establishing a strong web shadow will mean that you are able to present where you are now as people's first impression.
- **Build a positive present:** Don't try to mislead by creating lots of noise about yourself to push out negative mentions for the sake of it. Clumsy attempts to syndicate content and create a smoke and mirrors version of a web shadow can compound or confirm a negative impression rather than correct it. Worse still, someone would be within their rights to call you out in a public space online about your efforts to cover up the past. Better to focus on creating content and information about yourself that is real and useful.
- **Have an honest, clear response to questions about the past:** It may be that either online or in the real world people will naturally want to ask questions about your past, or question your integrity or judgement in the light of what has gone before. Develop a clear response that you can have to hand if this happens. Make it a conversation-closer rather than a debate-opener, perhaps, something along the lines of: 'What happened was sad and regretful. It is behind us all now.' Keep emotion out of the situation – don't be goaded into anger or over-apologising.

Reviewing progress

Now your plan is in place, remember to review progress from time to time. This could be as simple as re-looking at your web shadow, especially your Google results.

You should be able to sense how your efforts are going from your day to day interactions on the web. Measuring things may be a satisfying exercise though, and can give you ideas about how to work on developing your web shadow next.

Most social networks and web services will have some numbers or statistics you can take a look at and if you have a blog then you will be able to see some fairly sophisticated free measurement software (see Analytics section in Part III's *Things you need to know about... blogging*).

4. establishing your web presence

'Part of living in a networked society is learning how to accessorize our digital bodies, just as we learn to put on the appropriate clothes to go to the office.'

Danah Boyd,
Microsoft researcher and leading academic on online culture [25]

'...not everyone needs to spend a great deal of time and effort in becoming a [...] blogging celebrity, but there are sufficient number of easy to use tools available such that everyone can easily create an online presence. This doesn't really require you to give up any other activity, it is a byproduct of what you do anyway.'

Martin Weller,
Professor of Educational Technology at the Open University [26]

We can think of our web shadows as comprising three things:

1. Our presence: where we have established our own spaces or identity.
2. Our networks: the people and the places we connect to online, by 'friending' or linking to, and people and websites that link to us.
3. What is said about us: the other, most important element of our reputation.

This chapter deals with setting up and, to an extent, the maintaining of the first two elements of our web shadows.

[25] Boyd, Danah 'We Googled You: Should Fred hire Mimi despite her online history?' *Harvard Business Review*. June 2007 http://www.danah.org/papers/HBRJune2007.html

[26] http://nogoodreason.typepad.co.uk/no_good_reason/2009/07/in-a-comment-on-a-previous-post-my-colleague-chris-jones-argued-that-establishing-an-online-identity-wasnt-suitable-for-every.html

Where to establish presence and profiles
Must-haves and good-to-haves

From my point of view, we have two non-negotiable elements to establishing your web shadow: Facebook and LinkedIn. Both of these sites will appear in Google results against your name and (in the UK and North America, certainly) have become the places people go to look for information about people or to get in touch. You should not just set up profiles, but make sure that you have a network of contacts and are somewhat active in updating and managing your profile within them.

If you want to take as much control as possible of your web shadow, then you need to consider setting up the following:

A blog: Blogs are the best kind of personal website in my opinion. Low cost (or free) they are a great tool for connecting your web shadow, getting your thoughts out there and connecting with interesting people. Plus search engines love them. If you put some effort into a blog, it will probably rank first for your name or alias in Google.

Other social web presences: Any professional social networks are going to be a must, but you should also consider staking out profiles on social web services where you may want to become active later or that look interesting. You are more likely to get your preferred user name, alias or your own name if you do this with up and coming services.

Forums: As with social networks, if there are forums and communities relevant to your field of work, or personal interests, then you should establish profiles. Sometimes being a member will be necessary to search through conversations on such sites.

Life streams and profile aggregators: Lifestreaming services like FriendFeed (http://friendfeed.com) can be used to pull in all of your online activity, from your blog posts and status updates, to images or videos that you 'favourite'. There are a growing number of services which connect together your different web presences in a central location – the idea being that you give a central web address for people to get all of your contact details from. The .tel domain (web address) service (http://telnic. org/) is one to consider or chi.mp (http://chi.mp) which combines giving you a domain name with the ability to showcase feeds from other parts of your web presence, e.g. blog posts, photos from Flickr etc. Friendfeed and Posterous (http://posterous.com) are also classed as lifestreaming applications, which are worth looking at (more on these in Part III's *Useful tools for managing your web shadow*).

Whichever of these you decide to play with, ensure that you complete your Google Profile (http://www.google.com/profiles) which can also include the facility for people to contact you without giving them your email address.

How to establish profiles

Most websites where you establish a profile will have a simple process to guide you through registration. The following points need to be borne in mind for all of them, however.

Consistent naming

Choose a name – or just a couple – to use consistently across your networks. It will help you remember where they are, make listening (via Google Alerts, for instance) for mentions of yourself easier, and will make it easier for contacts and friends to recognise you. (I tend to be 'amayfield' in most networks, for instance; other people prefer an alias, like my friend oswald808.)

Profile/avatar image

Similarly, consider using a consistent image or photograph to represent you on different websites. (See the *About me…* chapter in Part III for more on creating interesting avatars.)

Mail settings

Check the settings to see how often the service will send you an email and about what. You can quickly overload your inbox with trivial message from social sites, if you aren't careful. Use one webmail address (such as Gmail) to manage all your accounts. This will keep all your information in one place and also makes it easier to get logged in if you forget your password.

Complete your profile

Try to complete your profile information, at least enough for friends to be able to tell it is you.

Making connections

Most services will offer to check your webmail or computer address book to see if anyone you know is using the service. You can also invite people who aren't members yet but who you think would enjoy it. Note: never 'invite all' on a social network (unless you really, really mean it). It is highly unlikely that you do want to connect with everyone you know in every space. There is also the distinct possibility that people will get annoyed if you are constantly inviting them to weird and wonderful websites that you don't actually visit again. That said, for places you decide you are going to be spending a lot of time, or that are central to your web shadow, you need to make sure you're connecting with as many of your real world contacts as possible.

Friends, connections and networking

While we are setting up our networks and thinking about inviting people to friend, connect with and follow us on the web, it is a good point to consider two related concepts: our *real* social networks and that thing they call networking.

Our social networks, of course, pre-date the web and exist independently of MySpace, Bebo or Hi5, to name but three of the online variety. Social networks are the people we know, that we meet and have some form of relationship with. They include our families, our close friends and colleagues. Each of these people has their own networks too, and they spread across the world, bit by bit, like the web itself, to connect every single one of us as part of the human species. Being connected, and as we have seen, being social, is very much part of what defines us as human beings.

Real friends and fake friends

The natural upper limit to the number of people in humans' social networks is believed to be about 150, based on the theory known as Dunbar's number, after the anthropologist who devised the theory[27]. Given that many people have more than that number of people in their Facebook profile, what are we supposed to make of this? One could go down the route of saying 'if God had meant us to be on Facebook he would have given us a higher Dunbar number', or we could ignore the whole thing and concentrate on how you think about large networks of friends and contacts on the web.

As usual, marketing expert Seth Godin has a rather pithy way of summing up all of this: how many people in your social network would you be comfortable guaranteeing a loan for? Here's a quote from a video of him in full swing at an American Express small business conference[28]:

> 'If you've got Facebook, you're probably my friend, because God knows I have enough of them. And it's worthless to you...It's worthless to have lots and lots of friends on Facebook: they're just people who didn't want to offend you by pressing the "ignore" button. And if you've got five thousand people following you on Twitter because you tell a dirty joke every couple of hours, that's not particularly useful for your business either.
>
> 'The internet is this giant cocktail party with all these people swarming around connecting as much as they can because they're keeping score...But one day when you need them to authorise a hundred thousand dollar contract, it doesn't matter.'

So he doesn't think that online relationships aren't real? Not at all.

> ' ...What matters is where are the real relationships [sic]? Now I have real relationships with thousands of people all around the world that I have never met. I can email people in New Zealand who would let me sleep in their living room for three days if I was in town. Because we have done stuff for each other, because we have exchanged worthwhile ideas.'

---

[27] http://en.wikipedia.org/wiki/Dunbar%27s_number

[28] Seth Godin on social networking: http://sethgodin.typepad.com/seths_blog/2009/07/four-videos-about-noise-social-and-decency.html

I know exactly what he means. So it turns out that the number of 'friends' you have on Facebook, or connections you have on LinkedIn, is not the measure of the value of your network.

Not that everyone agrees with Godin. Here's Guy Kawasaki on using Twitter singlemindedly as a marketing tool.

> 'I may get more value out of Twitter than anyone else on the planet because I use Twitter as a tool—specifically as a marketing tool— for my website Alltop and my book, *Reality Check*. If the concept of using Twitter in a commercial manner interests you, keep reading [this post]. If it doesn't, then you can continue to send and receive tweets about how cats are rolling over and the line at Starbucks.'[29]

Thinking about your networks

Dealing with large networks of contacts online means developing your own way of making sense of how you relate to people. Here's how I look at my networks:

- **Friends and family:** These are my most immediate relationships, the people I see (when I'm lucky) at least once a week or so. Would they pass the Seth Godin loan test? Absolutely. I'd drop what I was doing to help them if they needed me anytime.
- **Friends of friends:** People I know and like, but mainly in the context of relationships with those around me. We probably wouldn't arrange to go out for the evening together unless our mutual friend was there. If they asked us to guarantee a loan it would be odd, but we would certainly help them out in other ways.
- **Close colleagues and clients:** These are people I would call friends, but we probably don't socialise beyond work or business contexts. We would go out of our way for one another to connect each other with opportunities, introductions, give advice etc., however, the Godin loan test would be a stretch, wouldn't it? We would act as a reference, sure...

---

[29] How to use Twitter as a Tool, Guy Kawasaki – How to Change the World, December 2, 2008

- Contacts network: People we work with, have met a few times and can have a chat with. They may be friends of friends, or connected to our close colleagues, but we would find it hard to act as an employment reference perhaps, because we don't know them well enough to comment on their abilities.
- Latent network: These are people at the edge of my network – friends of friends of friends, perhaps, or people I've exchanged one or two comments and Tweets with online. We know *of* each other more than we know each other. We may still be connections on LinkedIn, Facebook or Twitter. I don't see these as 'low value' connections – the label 'latent' works for me on the level of 'potential friendships' or relationships that haven't started yet. It would be easy for me to ask to have a coffee to tell them about some business ideas, but I don't know them well enough to recommend me to clients.

Further reading

How we understand and cope with our expanding social networks is a fascinating area of online culture. If you want to dig into the issues around it a little deeper, take a look at this blog post by Danah Boyd http://www.zephoria.org/thoughts/archives/2009/07/28/would_the_real.html (use Google to look at more of her work too: it's brilliant).

5. public and private

'Every day my incoming email reminds me of the very words I wrote yesterday, last week or even months ago. It's as if the gotcha politics of Washington were being brought to bear on our everyday lives. Every time I finish an email message, I pause for a few seconds to reread it before I hit "send" just to make sure I haven't said something I'll later regret. It's as if I'm constantly awaiting the subpoena.'

Clive Thompson[30]

'Google never forgets.
'Of course, you don't have to be a drunk, a thief or a bitter failure for this to backfire. Everything you do now ends up in your permanent record. The best plan is to overload Google with a long tail of good stuff and to always act as if you're on Candid Camera, *because you are.'*

Seth Godin[31]

Can anyone be unGoogleable?

A couple of years ago, a journalist I know contacted me about an article he was working on for *The Times*[32]. He wanted to know how to get yourself *off* Google.

It was an interesting challenge. The company that I work for helps companies get their pages to the top of search engine results – I'd never heard of anyone wanting to disappear from them. Our head of search spent some time going through the options with him. Keeping yourself out of Google, it seems, is a full-time job – and much, much harder than trying to manage your reputation online positively.

It is hard to remove things that are said about you that you don't like on

---

[30] Thompson, Clive. 'The Honesty Virus', *New York Times*, 2004 http://www.nytimes.com/2004/03/21/magazine/21ESSAY.html?scp=20&sq=clive%20thompson&st=cse

[31] http://sethgodin.typepad.com/seths_blog/2009/02/personal-branding-in-the-age-of-google.html

[32] It's still online here: The title is How to be unGoogleable – but even by the introductory sentence it admits 'removing all traces of yourself from the internet is next to impossible'. http://technology.timesonline.co.uk/tol/news/tech_and_web/the_web/article4022374.ece

the web. If you are quick, you can delete or ask for things to be deleted that are inaccurate but even if owners of websites are helpful with this, the record of what has been said can exist in people's news readers, other places that RSS feeds end up or are syndicated to and can also be stored in the Google cache.

In public and on the permanent record

Not long after we say something online, or someone else says something about us, the Google bots come scurrying along and record it. This fact above all others should be a reminder to us that we are always on the record when it comes to the web.

Whether it is possible to remove particular pieces of data, apply to Google to have them scrubbed, bury them under a mound of positive pages and mentions of ourselves, the rule still applies:

You are always on the record online

What about private forums where Google can't crawl the pages? What about emails, text messages and instant messenger conversations? Well, while you are not actually on the public record in the moment you are using them, you should still regard yourself as on the record.

Digital data is a slippery, fluid thing that can easily find its way into all sorts of places. It is replicable easily and replicated often without the knowledge of anyone taking part in a conversation. Emails deleted by both sender and receiver can still be on a back-up somewhere, web pages browsed with 'private' settings, or via a proxy server to remove traces of your presence may still exist on your ISP or internet router's records.

Seriously, I'm not trying to make you feel nervous. Much of what you do or say electronically is effectively private, but my point is that you need to be in part prepared for the possibility that what you say or do online may become public. Corporate emails frequently become evidence in court cases, in some countries and cases the details of these have not only been discussed in court but released as part of evidence.

Data mining specialists – people whose software skills enable them to pull out the needles of meaning from mega-stacks of data – have exercised their skills in such infamous cases as the millions of emails between conspiracists in the Enron case[33]. Follow the link in the footnote to see network visualisations of emails between employees at Enron created by Kitware, Inc.

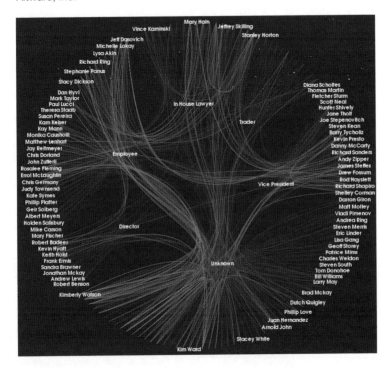

The best defence: pause before you publish

In order to ward off the possibility of damaging and negative content coming to light, we need to get into the habit of pausing before we publish (or post or send).

We don't need to be operating in the world of high finance or intelligence agencies to be worried about wrong data ending up in the wrong people's

---

[33] Enron Communications Graph http://www.visualcomplexity.com/vc/project.cfm?id=599

hands. An email mis-send or someone not having read the whole string of messages below theirs before they forward it on to someone who has been mentioned in an unflattering way can be highly embarrassing and damaging to relationships in business.

Sometimes telling a friend in confidence about a business success that's not yet public needs to have a caveat go along with it ('that's still very confidential'). Why? Because otherwise a well-meaning message on Twitter or Facebook can cause all sorts problems back at the office.

And that's just email! As the volume of data we create on the web increases we need to consider the implications of what we publish, say and do in public places. The simple act of changing a Facebook status or commenting on someone's wall has been cited in police cases as being the spark for violence in a domestic relationship.

Get into the habit of thinking about whether what you are saying is something you are happy for everyone to hear. If you are being contentious, that means being prepared to argue your point in public; if you are being critical of someone, that means being prepared to explain yourself to them.

If in doubt, don't press 'send'.

Is there any such thing as privacy anymore?

'The enlightenment idea of privacy is breaking apart under the strain of new social tools, new practices, new ways of being, new ways of doing things.'
Bill Thompson, journalist and technology commentator[34]

It may surprise you (it surprised me) to discover that the very idea of 'privacy' is a fairly recent one. Privacy as something we have a right to is something that is a subject of intense debate. There are those, such as Bill Thompson who feel that voluntarily giving up our privacy is something that will bring great benefits (if we don't let the government get too involved).

Others are raising the alarm about the amount of information we are giving away. Joshua-Michéle Ross has raised the spectre of a digital

---

[34] http://www.thebillblog.com/billblog/index.php/2009/02/27/lift09/

panopticon[35] that we are all voluntarily putting ourselves into by sharing so much information about ourselves.

In the age of social networks we find ourselves coming under a vast grid of surveillance – of permanent visibility. The routine self-reporting of what we are doing, reading, thinking via status updates makes our every action and location visible to the crowd.

It's not necessarily that the state is becoming Big Brother, but that we are all watching each other. As Ross puts it:

'the significance of status updates and location based services may not lie in the individual disclosure but in the significance of a culture that has become accustomed to constant disclosure.'

In taking my advice to 'pause before you publish' to its logical conclusion, will we become paralysed in every aspect our lives, unable to do anything that we think an imagined public of watchers would not approve of?

The answers, where we are going with all of this, are not clear, but as citizens of the web, even as we look after our web shadows and use the tools available to us to live more fulfilling, interesting lives, we need to be aware of the underlying trends and forces at work. If we end up in this particular nightmare scenario maybe it is not because a tyrannical government has removed our civil liberties, but because we have all given up our social liberties and surrendered our free will to the network.

Advertising and a new social contract

In 2007, Facebook was trying out a new advertising approach called Beacon. The idea was this: when you bought a product from a company participating in the scheme, news of that purchase would appear in your newsfeed telling all of your friends about it.

---

[35] http://radar.oreilly.com/2009/05/the-digital-panopticon.html. The panopticon, as Wikipedia puts it was, 'a type of prison building designed by English philosopher and social theorist Jeremy Bentham in 1785. The concept of the design is to allow an observer to observe (-opticon) all (pan-) prisoners without the prisoners being able to tell whether they are being watched, thereby conveying what one architect has called the "sentiment of an invisible omniscience."[1]'

Perfect! A way of generating advertising revenue for Facebook and harnessing the power of word of mouth at the same time. And people love to tell their friends about the things they have bought – what could possibly go wrong?[36]

Quite a lot, as it happened. One senior industry analyst wrote on her blog in horror about buying a Christmas present for her friend, which then appeared in her feed. Within hours there was an anti-Beacon movement thriving on Facebook and the wider web. Backpedalling and climb-downs from Facebook followed. Eventually in September 2009, it abandoned the service.

Facebook came under criticism from users again a year or so later when it revised its terms and conditions in a way which seemed to imply that *it* owned users' content (your photographs, for instance) even when they were removed. Once again, Facebook had to move quickly to allay people's concerns.

It's not just Facebook. Journalists, privacy campaigners and individuals online have joined forces to examine and criticise systems that tell ISPs more about who you are so that they can serve more relevant adverts as you visit different websites.

Advertisers and marketers (and yes, I am one of them) are in thrall to the social web at the moment. The reason is simple: old advertising models (TV and newspapers) are working increasingly less well as people's attention goes elsewhere and they get better at avoiding adverts.

There seems to be a new social contract between users of the web, advertisers and media companies emerging. If companies overstep the mark in terms of people's privacy there are enough people in the networks who will take notice, examine what is going on and raise the alarm.

Anonymity, aliases and pseudonyms

In the days when the web was like the Wild West, anonymity was the default approach to personal identity for many people. As one (anonymous, naturally) active user of the web since the early 90s put it to me: 'Having

---

[36] In case this is quoted out of context, it should be written in that mythical typeface the 'irony font'.

an alias, alternate identity was like having anti-virus software – it was just one of the ways that you protected yourself.'

For some people, having an anonymous or untraceable identity online is important for valid reasons – fear of persecution or personal safety if they are campaigning on a sensitive issue, for instance. Although I don't maintain any alternate identities myself, I can see a strong argument for the ability to do so being an important freedom for online citizens.

Another approach which many people use is to have a non-anonymous alternate identity. They don't hide who they are exactly, but equally they are choosing to have profiles which won't be immediately traced back to them by, for instance, an employer. This gives them an ability to 'be themselves' outside of their professional persona.

This semi-anonymity is more of a way of drawing a line between professional and personal lives online than a serious attempt to mask their identities (in fact they will still want to be found by friends). This may be an approach you feel comfortable with, but bear in mind that the essential law of online privacy – you're always on the record – applies still when you are using an alias.

Just as with trying to remove traces of yourself from Google, maintaining real privacy online can require a great deal of effort and technical know-how.

Note: It won't be the only time I recommend this website as a resource for information that can help in terms of your web shadow and wider online citizenship. For straightforward practical advice on security and privacy issues take a look at NGO Tactical Tech (http://tacticaltech.org) which provides information and support for social and political activists in countries where they may be at risk in expressing their views publicly. Especially useful is the Security in a Box (http://security.ngoinabox.org/) guide. If you find the information useful, you can make a donation by way of thanks.

Decision time: how public will you be?

It is time to make a decision: How open will you be on the web?

There are four main approaches I have seen people take in managing (for example) their Facebook presence and networking:

- **Personal-only:** Sometimes people have a personal-only social network on Facebook because their colleagues are not active online or don't see merit in connecting with each other. At the other end of the scale, some people who have big networks of professional contacts on Facebook have publicly stated their intention to 'un-friend' everyone but close friends and family, politely inviting their professional contacts to join them on LinkedIn instead.
- **Business-first:** Some people put their working lives before all else and live first and foremost as their professional selves. They seem to feel comfortable using Facebook as a more informal version of LinkedIn, essentially a business networking environment.
- **Blended/open lives:** Especially prevalent among early adopters, who have been living online for years, managing a web shadow across multiple platforms, 'blenders' as we might call them, are happy to live one life online, with family and friends seeing every conversation in the same way as business contacts and acquaintances. This approach is both simple (you know everything you say and do online is equally public) and shows confidence (what you see is very much what you get), but requires a conscious decision: that's it – you are now living your life in public.
- **Divided Facebook life:** More common, and what I suspect will become the default approach for web literate users of Facebook, is using the Groups feature in Facebook to define who of your friends sees what of your personal data, shared content and conversations on Facebook.

Our online privacy: here and now

As you can tell, I think it is important that we are aware of these issues. The web is expanding and affecting everything it touches, from the music industry to our love lives.

Take a look at the following points, and incorporate them into your planning or routines for managing your web shadow:

- Understand the privacy policies of websites before you publish information on them[37].
- Adjust your Facebook privacy settings and tell people you know about how to do this (see *Things you need to know about… Facebook* in Part III for more on this).
- Make sure your family and friends understand these privacy policies too.
- Be clear with yourself and those around you about what types of content you feel it is acceptable to share on the public web.
- Understand that if you email or post images and information, even on a private web space, there is a chance they may end up on the open web.
- If you tell people things that you don't want them to share online, make that clear to them.
- If you see images or content that you feel could damage your reputation ask people politely to remove them.
- If you feel that your privacy or rights are being breached in some way ask questions to your network and search for mentions of the issue. As we have seen, instant pressure groups can form and change big companies and even governments' minds about these issues very quickly.
- Become aware of your rights: there are laws in many countries which put restrictions on what data companies can hold about you and what they can do with it. Searches for 'data protection' or 'citizens data privacy' should show you government and NGO information on what your rights are.

---

[37] This article from ReadWriteWeb gives an interesting analysis of the privacy policies of some top websites in the US, which raises important issues. http://www.readwriteweb.com/enterprise/2009/07/15-top-privacy-policies-analyz.php

6. behaving yourself

Emerging etiquettes

'Interpersonal relations have had thousands of years to develop. Online, there's been no time.'

Seth Godin [38]

Howard Rheingold says that humans seem to suffer from 'rolling amnesia' when it comes to technology. It takes no time at all for us to become utterly accustomed to new technologies. So it was with mobile phones.

It is almost a decade and a half since I got my first mobile phone. Within a year most of my friends and family had them too. A couple of years later the company I worked for decided most people should have one and that the company would pay for it. We all went from a life where no one had mobiles to one where everyone did in just over a year.

Before mobiles you needed to agree to meet people at a certain time in a certain place. If like me you generally showed up slightly early or on time, it meant you spent a lot of time waiting for people.

Mobile phones were amazing. As they became cheaper to own and use everyone had to have one. There were too many reasons not to be without a mobile phone. For me, I wanted to be able to talk to clients and colleagues, stay in touch with my girlfriend during the busy week and be able to quickly and fluidly organise my social life.

In 2009, *WIRED* magazine published the slightly tongue-in-cheek 'How to Behave: New Rules for Highly Evolved Humans'[39]. It was a set of rules for the hyper-connected readers of the magazine, including such gems as, 'Don't Google Stalk Before a First Date' and 'Never Broadcast Your Relationship Status'. The jokes were mixed with a serious undercurrent: even the earliest adopters, the most digitally literate of us, are aware that we are negotiating a new set of rules for a world where we live part of our lives online.

---

[38] http://sethgodin.typepad.com/seths_blog/2009/07/social-norms.html

[39] http://www.wired.com/culture/lifestyle/magazine/17-08/by_index

Anomie

Sociologists have a word – actually two – for the difficulty we have understanding how we should behave in a time when every year or so we have a new communications channel added to our options for communication:

'...while people may be more accessible than ever, the norms for access are also more complicated than ever. Do I phone or email? Should I check instant messenger first to see if he is available, or perhaps look on Facebook? Does he check his cell phone messages? If I do not have his number who can I call to find out? Is he normally awake at this hour? Indeed, this may lead to a situation of anomie (or 'normlessness').'[40]

When even the choice of what communications medium to use is uncertain, what chance do we have of knowing the best way to behave when we start using it? It is a case of understanding two things:

- No one else does yet either. We will all work it out together over time.
- Our human social instincts and intuition should see us through until then.

Not passive, you are part of defining what is acceptable

Just as an etiquette emerged for mobile phone use in our business (we generally don't take calls in meetings any more) and personal (we generally switch our phone to silent in the cinema) circles, so it will emerge for the way we use the social web.

As etiquette emerges, it will be a result of us all using social media, experiencing and working through the issues and setting boundaries. Here are some suggestions for thinking about etiquette – but you will doubtless end up with your own sense of what appropriate behaviour is and isn't...

- **State your preferences in an open way:** Let people know how you feel. Photographs of our children are a good example of this – some

[40] http://individual.utoronto.ca/berniehogan/Hogan_NIEL_10-29-2008_FINAL.pdf

parents are happy to post photographs of their families on Facebook and photo-sharing websites with no privacy settings. Others are very uncomfortable about this, or simply not sure. When I'm posting pictures from our kid's birthday party, I don't know how the other parents feel about this, so I set the privacy settings to 'friends and family only' or something similar. If a family friend posts their pictures on the open web, I might explain to them that others are sensitive about this, and that maybe they would want to change the settings on those pictures.

■ Discuss your preferences, share experience: Telling the family friend about privacy settings on photos could really annoy and embarrass them if I present it in a prescriptive or patronising way. They don't have children themselves, so haven't encountered this very modern issue, and are relatively new to photo-sharing online (as are most people). How are they supposed to know? So it is best that I tell them about the different attitudes to this, and explain privacy settings to them – they may not even know about them. I can tell them about how I first dealt with the issue and offer to show where the privacy settings are on their photo site.

■ Be prepared to change your mind: Etiquette – norms of behaviour online – will emerge and continue to evolve because of negotiation. We need to approach discussions on these matters with our preferences clear but also with an open mind. It may well be that someone else's perspective on an issue can add to or change our own for the better.

Sensitive connected souls

So we know we are in public online, even when we feel like it is private, even when we think it is private. We know that in effect we are always on the record as well, even behind closed doors.

It is important to understand that our loved ones, friends and colleagues can all see what we are saying online. Everything we can do or say online can have an impact on others and we need to be sensitive to that.

Of course, while we want to be aware that speaking online is speaking in public, there are pitfalls of being overly self-conscious. Ideally, we should develop a mode of behaviour that is self-aware but not self-censoring. That means getting a thicker skin, that is to say not becoming less sensitive but able to take criticism or take on the risk of being criticised in public. It means we need to develop an emotional and intellectual self-confidence about what we do and say online.

As much as we need to be careful about what we say about ourselves we need to be conscious about what we are saying about others...

Eight things you probably shouldn't do in online networks

There do seem to be some cardinal sins, and as much as they are 'in the eye of the beholder' it would be remiss of me not to tell you about some of the behaviour that gets people angry online. Bear in mind that there are exceptions to all of these and that as you develop your own norms and etiquette in your networks, you may well challenge them.

1. Being spammy: Spam may be the original online sin. If we lift the lid on the pit of horrors that is our spam filter folder in our webmail we can see just how much. Every new communication platform on the web will at some point be tested by spammers to see if their business model will work.

   The term 'spammy' can be applied in situations other than someone in Miami trying to get you to start gambling, dating, buying prescription drugs or all of the above. Spamming is throwing too much irrelevant information out to too wide an audience.

Sometimes this can be inadvertent, the result of being tricked by an over-zealous marketer or just not reading the instructions carefully. Not so long ago, I had to issue a blanket apology to friends, colleagues and other contacts after signing up to a travel service that sent an invitation to join me to every address in my Gmail, a good couple of thousand, and some people got multiple mails. Very embarrassing, especially when you are supposed to vaguely know what you are doing online.

2. Acting privately in a public place: Knowing when to take conversations to a private place may be a part of etiquette to develop for yourself. Conversations between friends on Facebook walls or on Twitter can irritate others. Take it to email, Instant Messenger (IM) or some other more direct form of communication.

3. Oversharing: In 2008, 'overshare' was *Webster Dictionary's* word of the year[41]. A quick browse through Google results will reveal a catalogue of horror stories and some darkly humorous blogs dedicated to 'overshare'. The expression is used to describe people who have said too much or revealed a little too much online. Perhaps it was enough to say you were unwell, for example, rather than give detailed descriptions of your symptoms and share that attractive photo of your tonsils?

   Another reading of the idea of overshare would be sharing too many of your personal details. Obviously you wouldn't want to publish your home address, details of bank accounts and credit cards etc. because of the risk of identity fraud. Many people prefer not even to share their email addresses in public spaces, mainly because spammers can pick it up and add your address to their mailing lists.

4. Not linking back, or acknowledging sources: If you are writing or sharing something online you should say where you got it from, where possible with a link to the source. There are a number of reasons that this is good manners: it acknowledges the effort of the other person, gives them a link that helps with their search engine results and, perhaps most importantly, makes your post more useful for the reader.

5. Forgetting there's no 'irony font' online: For all its versatility, text-based communications are incredibly easy to read multiple meanings into. If you are reading something critical about yourself for instance, you will be adding in all sorts of meanings that may not be there. It's just how your brain works. Similarly, other people may easily get the wrong end of the stick when they are reading what you have said.

   The absence of an irony font is one of the reasons that I gave in and started using emoticons – little smiley faces that you create with

---

letters, e.g. :-) and ;-) for happy/funny and joking respectively, which I found so irritating for so long. They are like a safety feature in Tweets, texts and IMs that ensures the other person knows that what you are saying is meant in a friendly way. E.g. 'Well you would say that, wouldn't you?' might be construed as a bit huffy, whereas, 'Well you would say that wouldn't you? ;-)', makes it clear that you are joking – unless you are trying to use the emoticons ironically, in which case, frankly, you deserve to be misunderstood.

6. Posting in anger (or after a couple of drinks): Just no. Don't do it. Imagine everything you had ever said when you were angry or merry was indexed by Google. Yes, exactly...

7. Bullying and trolling: Aggressiveness and mocking is the default mode of conversation in some parts of the web: for instance, some video gamer forums or the comments on YouTube are basically a playground for trash-talking. Elsewhere we need to be sensitive to how our comments are interpreted. Not everyone has a thick skin and what you may think of as robust debate or a sensible dismantling of someone's argument can come across in a bullying way. Sometimes it is best to temper an argument with phrases like, 'I may be wrong', or 'I respect your position'. (I know not everyone will agree with this advice, but they are all idiots and should keep their petty, tawdry little opinions to themselves.[42])

'Trolls'[43] is the name given to people who are disruptive in unwelcome ways in an online space. It's a very childish and irritating way to behave and the best form of advice to people who experience it in groups is, 'do not feed the trolls' (abbreviated as DNFTT) which basically means if someone is only interested in stirring up trouble and provoking reactions in a group, ignore them (although feel free to report them to the site moderator to delete/ban them if you are moderating the group).

---

[42] See what I mean about irony fonts?

[43] Wikipedia has a good article on trolls if you want to know more: http://en.wikipedia.org/wiki/ Troll_%28Internet%29

8. Not respecting the privacy of others: We are clear then: living our lives in public is a new thing. We need to be careful, therefore, what we share about others in public. Want to comment on their Facebook wall about what they told you about their job last night in the pub? Sure they will appreciate that? Remember their boss and colleagues could be on Facebook too. Posting pictures of your child's school play on Facebook to show your work colleagues? What about the other people whose children are in the picture? Best to be careful with your privacy settings and keep it to a close group in that last example, but more widely, it is important to think twice about posting things that affect other people, and often best to ask them before you do so.

Being useful and synchronicity engines

You are just going to have to believe me when I tell you that I'm not a hippy, but I am going to talk about karma.

Networks are complex, adaptive systems. Even the simple social networks comprising our closest friends and family are complex. We cope with this by understanding the underlying behaviour of networks. We put good in, we tend to get good out. This essential truth has been expressed in religious terms – 'do unto others...' and in folksy proverbs ('reap what you sow', 'what goes around', etc.).

The core principle myself and my colleagues talk about for brands trying to succeed on the social web is the idea of earning reputation by being useful. A good way to gauge if what you are planning to do is a good idea is to ask: 'Is it useful?'

Six useful things to do on the web

Behaving well on the web will earn you a reputation and grow your web shadow at the same time. With 'useful' as our prime mover in this, here are some practical things that you can do to make yourself useful about the place...

1. Listening: The act of listening is highly social: conversations begin with listening. Listening to what people are saying or reading their

posts on a blog or in a forum adds value to that network in a small way. For instance, the fact that you have spent attention is registered in the data about that post and makes it more likely that others will take note later on. It is good to join in a conversation, but relax and don't feel you have to until you are ready. Listening is a good start.

2. **Rating, commenting, sharing and thanking:** Joining in conversations and adding to them doesn't mean that you have to stride centre stage right away. You can begin in small ways. If you enjoy an article or post, say so in the comments or rate it. It is very rewarding to the author to see the reactions (good and bad) and gives them the motivation to do more similar work. Likewise, where there are share buttons to let you post to Delicious, Facebook or Twitter, if you think something is interesting then sharing it is a very useful thing to do: it is a reward/approval signal to the creator and will bring it to the attention of a few more people in your network who might not otherwise have heard about it.

3. **Sharing your work:** So much of our work, our thinking, creations and conversations go to waste needlessly. You don't need to have the definitive or most ground-breaking piece of work in your field to publish it online – it doesn't even need to be finished. My favourite example of this is presentations we give to our colleagues about an area we are interested in or a brief presentation we might give at a conference or industry event. So much effort goes into these and then they simply languish on a server. Why not publish them on SlideShare and let people know about them?

For example I wrote a presentation for the Word of Mouth Marketing Association (WOMMA) a couple of months ago. Something like a hundred people chose to watch the live webinar. I published it on SlideShare and linked to it from my company blog, from Twitter and told a few people who would be interested about it and a couple of days later a few thousand people had chosen to look at it, leaving encouraging comments and a few had added it to their Favourites. They included peers from the marketing world, but also some academics. And they were from all around the world. Not all of the presentations I have put online get that much attention, but I will make sure that all my decent ones go up from now on. For half an hour's extra work, that presentation earned a lot more attention because it was useful to share it and because it was in a useful format, it was in a place where people *could* share it.

4. Answering questions: Services like Yahoo! Answers and the Answers section in LinkedIn are good places to share your particular areas of expertise, sometimes referred to as 'knowledge markets'. You may very well be surprised with how much demand. Remember to answer clearly and link to resources that can help people out. (Your Yahoo! Answers profile can be connected to your web shadow's other locations, if you start developing a strong profile there).

5. Forming groups and communities: Becoming the organiser, convenor or administrator of an online group can be a useful thing to do. Be sure there is a clear need for it and have an idea of who will be your co-organisers or first members if you do.

6. Giving things away: The copyright and intellectual property industry's prevalence in old media has trickled down some strange ideas to us about creating value through copyright. Unless you are actually in the business of selling music, videos or other media, and especially as an individual, giving things away (with some conditions attached) can create a lot more value. See the story about the e-book I created with some colleagues at iCrossing below, but in the meantime take some time to understand how alternatives to copyright like Creative Commons licensing can work[44]. My preference is to licence my blog, presentations and photographs under a Creative Commons Attribution licence, which means, basically, that anyone can re-publish or re-use those works as long as they acknowledge me or my company (depending on who I have created it for originally) as the creator.

---

[44] Start with **http:creativecommons.org.uk** or **http://creativecommons.org/about/ what-is-cc** for explanations of how to use the licences.

Your web shadow at work

If you work for an employer, you'll need to be aware of some issues both around how you behave on the web and how you grow and manage your web shadow. These are guidelines only, as the circumstances will obviously vary between companies and organisations.

After years of stories about organisations' knee-jerk reactions to people's personal use of the web, I think we are beginning to see many companies developing a more enlightened view of how their people are using social media. Where the tone has often been about managing risk and pulling employees into line, many are now seeing the opportunities that lie in having a social web-literate workforce.

Web use/social media policies

Many organisations will have policies about how employees use the web. If they don't it is probably best to take general rules for conduct in the workplace and apply to them to how you operate online. If you are blogging or creating content and are connecting yourself to your employer in your biography it is a good idea to have a disclaimer in place noting that the opinions expressed are yours and not your employer's. You may also want to let your boss know that you are blogging and what you intend to write about and, if necessary, reassure them that you won't talk about anything that would compromise the company's reputation.

Areas that could get you into hot water include:

■ **Disclosing sensitive information:** This is the one that might get you fired fastest. If your company is publicly listed or you work for a government organisation, this is the kind of thing that means the organisation could get into trouble. Expect lawyers or ombudsmen to descend on you like a ton of bricks. If you aren't sure what sort of information disclosure could get you in trouble: ask. Or just steer clear of talking about these subjects. If you work in a highly regulated sector like finance or pharmaceuticals it is probably best to stay away from contentious areas and find other things to talk about. Unless you are a compliance officer or lawyer, in which case these things may be what you want to be talking about most of the time...

■ **Complaining about your workplace/co-workers:** Seriously. Just not a great idea. Unless you are dying to become the next 'I got fired on Facebook' story for the BBC[45].

■ **Attacking a brand:** If you are slating service from a company you have had dealings with on a personal basis, you might want to check that your firm's not about to land a contract with them or that they are not a top customer.

[45] http://news.bbc.co.uk/1/hi/england/essex/7914415.stm

7. dealing with bad things online

Like any other part of life, any town, city or community, there are some bad apples, some bad people out there. It used to seem that what the mainstream media mainly talked about when it came to the internet was the porn, the criminals, the dangers.

As the web has grown to include mainstream media, and most of our lives, we have come to understand that there is much more. Good people, good places, outnumber the bad, just as they do in the real world.

Just as the postal service brought the poison pen letter, and the telephone brought prank callers and other grim tactics of harassment, so the web has its fair share. This chapter will introduce some of them, and suggest ways to deal with them. But as they say on Crimewatch[46]: don't have nightmares...

Abuse and criticism

We've spoken a little bit about trolls. But what happens when someone starts being abusive to you in an online forum?

Is it really abuse?

First of all, take a step back and breathe. Are you really being abused, or is this a strongly worded argument? You may be on a blog or forum which seems civilised, but certain topics (contentious religious and political issues, sporting allegiances and, well, Apples v. PCs) will bring hardcore holders of certain views flocking to a website, bringing a way of expressing themselves which may well sound abusive or troll-ish.

Who are they?

If someone is posting anonymously, try to get an idea of who they are. If it is your blog they are on, you may be able to see from the analytics where their IP address is from or their email address. If the website they are posting from seems to be theirs, take a look at who is hosting it using a service like

---

[46] A UK crime reconstruction TV show

WhoIsHostingThis.com (http://www.whoishostingthis.com/) and whether the domain name is registered in their name (http://www.whois.net/).

Does it matter?

If someone wants to be offended, they're only ever a search or a couple of clicks from something that will raise their hackles. Ask yourself what people who matter to you will think when they see the comments. In most cases, ignoring them (remember 'don't feed the trolls') is the most sensible course.

But if someone is being directly abusive to you or is being offensive on your blog or in a space you are running (like a forum), then you have every right to take action by blocking them, deleting their comments, or, if applicable, reporting them to the people who run the site ('report abuse' buttons are common).

Online bully (a.k.a. cyberbullying)

Bullying using web media and mobiles (usually text messages) is an extension of the despicable practice of bullying in the real world. It can feel even more intimidating for some victims because it feels as if there is no safe refuge – the abuse follows them wherever they are. The phenomenon has been highlighted by some depressing cases where children and young people have committed suicide in part due to bullying via texts, email, IM and social networks (in one bizarre instance in the US, one bully was revealed to be a parent of the victim's friends).

We will differentiate bullying from abuse by saying that bullying is a persistent campaign of abuse by an individual or group or an individual. It can include not just direct communications but also the publishing of hurtful and embarrassing content about the victim in public places.

These abusive practices are very real and effective and we need to take them seriously. Besides the tragic instances of young people taking their own lives, we can see evidence of abuse in the use of text messaging and emails by both sides in the recent conflict between Israel and Palestine. In the context of a warzone it is called psychological warfare.

Dealing with bullying online

- **Ignore it:** Bullies are often looking for a reaction. Try to be in the mindset that this is an inconvenience and don't be baited into responding.
- **Keep a record:** Times, numbers, screen-grabs of websites and so on should all be recorded. If the bullying continues, you are gathering evidence to show to website owners, teachers or even the police.
- **Block email addresses/telephone numbers/IP addresses:** A practical measure is simply to block the offender from contacting you by email, text message or to prevent them from accessing your website. Phone companies, ISPs, and social network hosts will usually have a straightforward way of doing this if you contact them. If you want to bar someone from your blog or website you may need to seek some technical assistance.
- **Contact service providers:** If social networks or mobile networks are being used to deliver abuse, you can contact them direct. Most should act quickly to help the victim. Changing your phone number or email address may be a quick way to resolve matters.
- **Don't confront bullies:** Most advice from charities (see links below) says not confront suspected bullies.
- **Contact authorities:** If it is your child who is being bullied, contacting their school early on may be a good idea. Where bullying is serious, you may need to contact the police for advice and support.

Further reading on cyberbullying:
Childline (UK) advice on bullying: http://www.childline.org.uk/Explore/Bullying/Pages/Bullying.aspx
Digizen http://www.digizen.org/
Beat Bullying http://www.beatbullying.org/
Anti-bullying Alliance http://www.anti-bullyingalliance.org.uk/

Take downs and taking legal advice

If there is content (images, video or text) about you on someone's website that you feel is damaging to your reputation the best thing to do is politely ask them to take it down. If this doesn't work, it may be time to talk to a lawyer.

Check first that you don't have legal insurance or access to a legal helpline through credit cards, household insurance or professional associations. Failing that find a lawyer at a rate you can afford and ask their advice about whether you have grounds to get the offending item taken down.

A letter from a solicitor will often bring people to their senses. After that it can get very expensive, and it will be a case of how much you think removal of the content is worth to your reputation.

Again, try to keep perspective here: if you are the first/best source of information about yourself on the web and you have a healthy web shadow full of evidence of your being a generally good person, it may not matter too much.

You should also note that clumsy, threatening attempts by email and letter to have someone take down content about you may do more harm than good. The more you protest the more attention you may attract to precisely the thing you wanted removed. Many's the blogger who has gathered support around them by publishing letters and emails from corporations threatening them.

Dealing with your own mistakes

Never mind the cyber bullies and the trolls, sometimes our worst enemy online is ourselves. What happens when we screw up? Let's say you've posted something accidentally, said something that you instantly regretted or instantly interpreted in a way that had never occurred to you (but with immediate, painful hindsight, probably should have). What do you do then? I'd suggest:

- **Moving quickly:** Seconds can count in these matters. If it is a case of an accidental posting, delete it immediately. Also, think about where else it might have gone. If it is a case of a status update or post where you posted the wrong thing or phrase, post the right one straight away.
- **Apologising properly:** If you have something to apologise for, do it properly when it becomes clear that an apology will be required. That means in a personal tone of voice, as it were, rather than a formal one, and without blaming others or going overboard on extenuating

circumstances. It also means not waiting until you have no alternative but to apologise. If there is a chance of legal action, however, you might want to take professional advice (communications as well as legal) as soon as possible.

- **Keeping an eye on the aftermath:** Pay very close attention to what happens next. Keep an eye on blogs and the rest of the web via Google and probably Twitter Search (this covers things on Twitter as they happen, whereas there is a delay on Google) as well as any other search engines or within the network. Try to keep things from escalating by being responsive and getting involved in the conversation.

Get a thicker skin
Daring to be wrong

Seriously, I think it is an English or British thing (so other nationalities may skip to the next section) but we don't like being told we're wrong. We especially don't like it happening in public. For some reason, being criticised was my biggest personal fear when I started blogging.

Quite simply, you need to get over it.

The web is a conversation, as they say. It is also a raging debate a fair amount of the time. And that means dusting off those debating skills and reminding yourself what the cut and thrust of an honest argument is all about. It is OK to be wrong, it's fine to hold two conflicting ideas in your head. You get into conversations to get closer to the truth, and if that means realising that your previous position was wrong, that's all to the good. At least you found out now.

This photo makes me look silly! So what?

Having spent a nice amount of time over the last few years hanging out with bloggers, web experts and assorted online folk, I have more than my fair share of silly photos of me on the web. This one was taken by Mafe De Baggis[47] in a bar after a conference in Udine, Italy.

I look ridiculous. But that kind of goes with the territory when you're me. I had to get over it.

Mafe might even have been so kind as to remove the photo if I had asked. But would it be worth it? I'm not running for high office. I don't think I'll lose any jobs because I blow off a little steam pulling funny faces in a bar after a couple of beers.

We've talked a lot in this book about how to present the best image of yourself on the web, to try and manage your web shadow. What is equally

---

[47] Published on flickr under Creative Commons licence. http://www.flickr.com/ photos/36521965377@N01/2268399841/

important as understanding what is within your control however, is understanding what is not.

Our attitudes to what 'looks professional', what is a proper way to appear, will most likely need to shift. If we reject every graduate job applicant our due diligence finds photographs of dancing on tables in the student union bar, we will be wasting a lot of opportunities to get the best people hired. I liked this from the *Economist*'s 'World in 2009'[48] that imagines everyone having to loosen up and reel in their hypocritical standards for politicians because of just how much more open our lives are becoming:

> 'Perhaps, when dirt on almost everybody becomes readily available, politics will lose its hypocritical, moralistic tone. Having the modern-day Javerts in human resources trawling through one's every online utterance could hammer home the point that everyone's closet has a skeleton, if only you can reach far enough in. That could make people realise that politicians, too, are only human, and make them more forgiving of minor transgressions. Or perhaps the very idea will merely convince a future employer that your correspondent is unemployably naïve.'

Identity hijacking
What is it?

This is your identity speaking. Hijackers have just taken over and our reputation is being held hostage...

OK, don't panic. Identity hijacking is basically a new phrase which describes someone impersonating you on a social network or elsewhere online. It may be a practical joke or a form of harassment, for instance. CafeMom (http://www.cafemom.com/), a popular US community, says that it has seen some of this behaviour and thinks of it as Trolling 2.0, a new form of troublemaking.

If you have set up your web shadow it should be fairly easy to counter this by making it clear to people that this is not you. Staking out your profile on social networks is another way of protecting against this kind of attack.

---

[48] Everybody Does It: The Economist: January 2nd 2009

Contacting the service provider (moderators, hosts, owners of service) where you are being impersonated should give you a way to resolve identity hijacking reasonably quickly. In the meantime don't respond to every twist and turn of the troublemaking impersonator – but do make sure that you keep a close eye on email and other communications to clear up any misunderstandings. Post a matter of fact disclaimer on your blog and other presences if the impersonator is getting some attention – otherwise ignore them until the matter can be resolved. Remember, like any bully or troll, what they want most of all is to get a reaction.

Further reading

What Poppy Did: How to get your photo removed from a porn site http://poppyd.tumblr.com/post/149501794/how-to-get-your-photos-removed-from-a-porn-site

Fake social network profiles: A New Form of Identity Theft in 2009, ReadWriteWeb: http://www.readwriteweb.com/archives/fake_social_network_profiles_a.php

part III:
practical
advice for
digital lives

We have already discussed that I like to think of this section of *Me and My Web Shadow* as the Haynes Manual[49] section of the book, but then it occurs to me that Haynes may well, at some point, publish their own book on how to use social computing tools and do a far more comprehensive job than I can do here. Let's hope so and in the meantime regard this as a while-we-wait-for-Haynes guide to using them.

---

[49] Note for non-UK readers: Haynes is famous in Britain for its series of books with clear instructions on how to service your particular model of car. Recently they have applied the same principles to books (aimed at men) on how to care for a baby or be a good father (I own both of these and, joking aside, they are excellent).

1. workflow: fitting web shadow management into your routine

Of all the things most people need right now, extra work is not one of them. Even as you are reading *Me and My Web Shadow* a part of your mind may be thinking: 'All sounds great – but where will I get the time?'

There is good news and better news on this front coming to you in this chapter. First, by incorporating some tools and techniques into your working day and your workflows around specific tasks, managing your web shadow should take up very little extra time. Second, the tools and services which can help you manage your online presence can displace other less efficient work practices.

Throughout Part III we will be looking at some of the wonderful, mostly free, tools and web services that can help you manage your web shadow. But first I want to issue a web shadows health warning about technology use.

Who's in charge: you or the machine?

It is not all rosy when it comes to our use of technology, is it? There is a danger of addiction, becoming slaves to the machines, that we are at risk of being drawn into.

Two of the great communications technologies of the last 10 years or so have become universal and commonplace: email and mobile phones. Once we understood the benefits and began to use them *en masse*, a lot of people seemed to develop problems with both of these technologies. Mobile phones would be used inappropriately and compulsively: bosses and co-workers seemed to suddenly feel it was OK to call you at any time of day, at the weekends or while you were on holiday. The phone went everywhere and was checked liked a reflex. Conversations would be interrupted, voicemail and texts checked constantly.

Similarly, emails are a blessing that came with a hidden curse. As well as giving us an incredibly efficient way of communicating with each other, we soon began to evolve dangerous new bad habits that started robbing us of time. Take, for example, 'CC-Syndrome', where people feel compelled to copy in huge numbers of people into messages meaning that a simple communication suddenly becomes spam and can spawn multiple threads that become increasingly difficult to understand.

Eventually, email starts to break and we have to start coming up with new ways of dealing with it. Partly technology comes to the rescue with new filters.

When you get 400 emails a day, you cannot possibly read them all and have a productive working life, unless your job is actually answering emails and that alone. Outside of customer service roles, that's a rare, rare thing indeed.

CrackBerry Syndrome – people's addiction to checking and communicating via email – brought a sinister synthesis of mobiles and emails that was hard for many to resist. Email, text message and BlackBerry® abuse seem very similar to video game addiction when you look closely. The reward centres in users' brains fire off little puffs of serotonin each time they clear another email, receive another text or compulsively fire up their BlackBerry® — every time that little light starts flashing.

While we sneer at the 'pointless' obsession of video gaming and worry about younger relatives who seem to be hooked on playing them for hours on end, there's something about the CrackBerry addict concept that implies status, or at least the fantasy of being so important, so needed, that email cannot be left to lie in an inbox for more than a few moments.

Declare your independence

Don't be impressed by the out of hours email from someone that says and affects little other than to say, 'I am here, I'm online, I'm putting in the hours.' It's a rubbish, boring ineffective game that achieves very little at a great personal cost, and at a cost to those around them too.

We have to take responsibility for our own lives when it comes to technology. Just because there are thousands of emails in your inbox when you come back from holiday does not mean that you need to answer them all.

Critical self-appraisal is required to understand when we are becoming addicted to the video game of email or mobile communications. And yes, the same disease can befall users of social networks and other Web 2.0.

In my personal experience of web tools I have become semi-addicted to various services for periods of time. I don't think it's necessarily bad while you are learning to use a new thing online to become temporarily obsessed with it – it can help you focus for long enough to learn it properly. It is just important to recognise when you are beginning not to get very much out of what you are doing in terms of learning or other benefits and decide to move on at that point.

Completism v. Flow

Our cultural bias for work and study is towards completing things. We perceive a virtue in reading the newspaper from start to finish each day or in the report begun, carried through and completed by an individual or team. These are ways of thinking and behaving which may change as we begin to understand the possibilities of working with the web.

Ideas like standardisation, definitive editions of books, cross-referencing and indexes all seem natural to us now, but they were ideas which emerged with the technology of the printing press. References and bibliographies actually started as a form of marketing by printers – a print based version of Amazon's 'People who bought this book also bought' feature, perhaps.

The idea of accuracy in a text and proofreading didn't exist in the same way before print. As we begin to work and live with the web ever more it will change the way we think about things and the way we work.

Perhaps soon completing things won't be considered as valuable as it was before. When rich people in the 17th century displayed their sophistication and wealth with a big personal library, they would have read everything in them at some point (or claimed to, or hoped to).

When my young children sit down at the family computer and open a web browser they instantly have access to more information than any scholar did before the 1990s. Neither of them has a hope of ever reading all that information. They will need to come to terms with that early on.

Their success – intellectually, culturally, academically and professionally – will most likely be based on their ability to filter, find, curate and make sense of some of that information. They will need to understand when to leave a trail of links, when to go with the flow, how to develop a network of other people with similar interests to collaborate with informally, formally, on and off and when they need them.

Thinking of this reminds me of Twitter a little: it is a gloriously rewarding communications medium. If you had nothing else to do and had developed a strong network of interesting people to follow on Twitter (see *Things you need to know about… Twitter* later in this section for a fuller explanation of Twitter) then you could easily spend all day reading it, following interesting links, talking to other users on it and re-Tweeting (re-publishing) the best of what you found.

At the end of that day, you would have had read an awful lot of interesting things, had some interesting conversations and, quite possibly, have had a great deal of fun. What you would have achieved would be contained to that network though, to that experience. You wouldn't have done anything else.

Which would be fine, if you didn't need to earn a living as well. It would also be fine if you were trying to learn Twitter, develop your Twitter literacy, as it were. In everyday life, however, we need to know when to turn off Twitter, and when to dip into it: when to connect to our networks.

Stowe Boyd[50], the technologist and thinker, describes having learned to have communications channels open to your networks while also getting on with other work as a state of flow. This is a great trick to be able to pull off, but it does take skill, a level of literacy and some personal discipline, I would argue. Howard Rheingold talks about the importance of being able to focus our attention on a single thing for long periods of time, like a 'spotlight'[51]. In that analogy, I guess we could think about 'flow' as being like diffusing our attention, spreading it out, and seeing what we can see.

---

[50] http://en.wikipedia.org/wiki/Stowe_Boyd
[51] Howard Rheingold, Smart Mibs blog http://bit.ly/8ad92a

Immediate and emergent benefits for your workflow

It can take some time to fully learn how to use web tools and services to their best potential. The good news is that many of these services re-pay you with benefits straightaway, even as you are figuring out how the more advanced features work.

Think of any social computing or web tool as having both immediate and emergent benefits. The immediate ones should keep you using it while you learn it and the emergent benefits come like 'power-ups' in a video game as you move on up through the levels.

Take for example, Delicious, which we go into in some detail later on. Delicious is a social bookmarking service. Instead of adding a website to your 'Favourites' or 'Bookmarks' on your web browser, you can click a button on your web browser and save it to your Delicious account. Rather than save it in a folder, you add some words, or 'tags', to describe it. For instance, if you are bookmarking the *Me and My Web Shadow* web page (www.meandmywebshadow.com since you ask) then you might add 'career', 'personal', 'privacy', 'reputation', 'networking', 'book', 'web', 'how to' and 'web shadows'.

When you want to see the page again, you press the Delicious button on your browser and from your personal Delicious page you can look for it by date, search for the name of the site, or enter one of the tag words you used to describe it.

The *immediate benefits* of this are that it solves a number of problems with 'Favourites' or 'Bookmarks' folders:

- **Losing Favourites:** When a computer died on me or I changed machines in the past, I would sometimes lose my Favourites. With Delicious, that no longer happens.
- **Seeing Favourites on different machines:** Having a work computer and a home computer can be annoying if you want to access your Favourites and they are split between two machines. With Delicious I can log on to my account from anywhere on any machine.

- Organising Favourites: My folder system was a mess. Where to save things? Where *did* I save things? Saving and finding bookmarks was a little irritating. Delicious's tags solve that – tags are a much more versatile way of saving and the search options in Delicious make it relatively easy to find things again just when I want them.

The longer you use it, the more you learn about it and the more useful it becomes. After a few months of using Delicious, it had become a habit and I was tagging anything I read that I thought would be useful. Now, I effectively have an online personal database of thousands of pages that might come in handy sometime.

Great. That's that solved, then. Why isn't everyone in the world using Delicious already? But there is more to Delicious. Much more. As you use it more it reveals *emergent benefits*.

It is a *social* bookmarking service after all. Your Delicious bookmarks are visible to anyone who cares to take a look. It means when you search for 'privacy', 'web' and 'how_to' (many people use 'howto' on Delicious as well) you will find not the pages you thought were interesting on this topic, but everything that the few million users of the service bookmarked (take a look at http://delicious.com/tag/privacy+how_to). This can be very useful indeed.

In fact, if you take a look at my Delicious account you can see most of the research for this book (mainly I have been using the tag 'personal' for pages I thought were interesting and will be organising a set of useful links related to this book at http://delicious.com/amayfield/webshadows as soon as I have finished writing and before you finish reading). Useful, eh? Well if you want to join in just sign up and if you see anything you think will be useful to the rest of us (me and the other readers of *Me and My Web Shadow*) just tag it 'webshadows' and we can all see it.

Using the RSS feed (remember those?) that Delicious generates for the 'webshadows' tag page, I can create a page on www.antonymayfield. com/webshadows that will publish them all on that web page too.

There were a lot of people on Delicious who helped me write this book – and they didn't even know it. Using the 'Network feature', I follow people like Howard Rheingold (http://delicious.com/hrheingold), Jeff Jarvis (http://delicious.com/buzzmachine), Robb Montgomery (www.delicious.com/vizeds), who trains journalists on using new media, and Ewan McIntosh (www.delicious.com/ewan.mcintosh) an education and digital expert who works for 4IP, the Channel 4 fund that invests in interesting new media companies.

Writing aside, Delicious and Twitter are two of the most useful tools in my day job, besides the Google Search Engine, for all sorts of tasks, from making travel plans to writing a proposal or exploring new ideas in the media and marketing industries. My colleagues and I use it much more than email for sharing ideas, too.

Using a tool like Delicious will save you time, then, both in terms of a more efficient way of bookmarking the web and helping with research and potentially staying on top of developments in your field more effectively (others tell you what the most important things are to read).

We'll go into more details about other tools you can use to both manage your web shadow more effectively and work more efficiently in *Useful tools for managing your web shadow* later in Part III. Here are a couple of examples – you will discover many more for yourself...

News readers

- **Immediate benefits:** News readers (RSS Readers) like Google Reader and NetNewsNow can greatly speed up your reading of news, industry publications and blogs. You subscribe to pages you are interested in (say BBC News, the Telegraph's business news and some blogs) and know when there are new articles or posts for you to read.
- **Emergent benefits:** News readers often include features that will let you share the articles you are reading with others via email, Delicious, Twitter and other online services. So quickly scanning your reader, choosing a couple of articles and sending them to others makes you more useful in your network, by helping others find interesting content online.

Document collaborating

- **Immediate benefits:** Services like Google Docs and wikis allow you to create documents and share them online with others while you are working on them. This removes the 'versioning' nightmare of multiple versions of a single document being edited by different people on an email changing before being sent back to a hapless author for editing. Saves hours of stress.
- **Emergent benefits:** Creating a document can become a social activity in itself, a way of turning a conversation into action: a plan for an event, a manifesto, a vision statement, a petition, a brainstorm. Documents can become social spaces (where we meet and talk) and social objects (the reason we are talking, the focus).

Sharing documents and presentations

- **Immediate benefits:** Posting documents you are prepared to share publicly on services like Scribd, SlideShare and Google Docs does two things immediately: first, it means all your colleagues and peers can get access to the document when they want rather than having to keep it in their over-stuffed email inbox or saving it to their 'To Read' folder that may never get opened again and second, it means it is backed up and easy for you to find.
- **Emergent benefits:** What is incredible about sharing documents online with the wider web is the power it adds to the 'synchronicity engine' element of the web. You never know who will find it useful – people from other industries and sectors, potential collaborators and clients or even employers. Also, once the presentation or document is published it becomes very portable and versatile – you can very easily embed it in a blog post, and share it on Facebook, LinkedIn, Twitter and other social spaces.

Checkpoints and checklists

However you work, whether you're a pen-and-paper priority lister, a GTD[52] devotee or an edge-of-chaos free spirit, it's a good idea to put in place some routines and markers to make sure that you stay on top of your web shadow management.

A bare minimum would be a six-monthly reminder to yourself to take an hour to review profiles on LinkedIn, Facebook and other sites that are important to you, update biography information and cross-check that your contacts are up to date.

Beyond that, and especially if you want to develop your web shadow and wider online reputation, you should consider keeping a checklist or set of checklists to run through. If you are just interested in the basics of managing your web shadow just make a list for every few months (six at most), to review that your profiles are still current and you're aware of what your web shadow looks like. For a more active approach to developing your online presence, think about booking reviews in every month, and add some kind of checkpoint to your weekly and daily routines.

---

[52] GTD stands for Getting Things Done, a book about managing your work by David Allen.
http://en.wikipedia.org/wiki/Getting_Things_Done

Here's a sample checklist of things you might consider as a starting point:

Six months	Check your web shadow	• Background check yourself: check misspellings, your company and peers on Google, other search engines, social networks and other services (e.g. Twitter). • Look at the top 5 & 10 sites especially, and later results.
	Security	• Change passwords. • Review privacy settings (these may have changed, along with privacy policies on some networks). • Back up photos, contacts, bookmarks and other online content.
	Personal information	• Review biography, update photograph. • Check profiles/biographies on profiles/your presence.
	Contacts	• Re-submit contacts files from webmail and computer's address book to LinkedIn/other social networks.
	Keep up to date	• Search for websites with key industry/sector terms. • Book your next web shadow review session in your diary.
Monthly	Check your web shadow	• Check your Google shadow.
	Security	• Change core passwords. • Check family/close friends' privacy settings.
	Shareable content	• Review your work from the past month – is there anything that can be shared? • Is there anything that can be adapted as a brief blog post with some notes on your thoughts and experiences?
	Contacts	• Re-submit contacts files from webmail and computer's address book to LinkedIn/other social networks.
Weekly	Check your web shadow	• Review industry/sector groups in core networks.
	Contacts	• Check who has viewed your profile on LinkedIn.
Daily	Respond	• View any Google Alerts. • Respond to contact invitations/alerts from social networks etc.

2. about me: creating and maintaining your web shadow content

Building a web shadow content toolkit

Some people enjoy talking about themselves and can give you a one hundred word run-down on their qualities and achievements at the drop of a hat. For the rest of us it is best that we have a prepared statement or at least a list of prompts to hand.

Despite having written biographies for people for years in PR, I still find it very hard to write about myself in a concise, interesting way.

Set up a folder on your computer with a set of personal content that you can use without having to think about it, or worry about it, every time there is a part of a web form that asks you to.

You can either fill this up as you go along creating profiles and exploring your network, or you can bite the bullet and get at least the basics in place all at once.

Photographs

You will need to have at least one portrait photograph of yourself at high resolution.

How formal it is will depend a lot on your personality and the profession that you are in. However, if in doubt, go for the suited, little-bit-serious approach – you can always add more personality-laden images to your personal gallery.

If you are lucky enough to have had a publicity shot taken of you by the company, see whether you can get permission to use it in your personal profiles as well. Very often employers have no issue with this, but check with the marketing or PR team before you go ahead in case the photographer holds copyright. Even if they do, usually all you need is permission.

The other option is DIY. With the spread of high quality digital cameras you may well know someone who fancies their photographic skills. Get them to take a lot of pictures of you in a single sitting if you can – it is much more likely that you will get lucky and get a shot which is presentable.

Just as with a biography, get a trusted friend or colleague to take a look as a final test that the photo is good. Very often, we are the least qualified people in the world to say whether a picture of us is a good one or appropriate for public use.

From a technical point of view, make sure you have a small version of the file in a JPEG format and a larger, high definition one for other purposes. You can use free image editors like The Gimp[53] to do this.

Lastly, consider the following tips:

Use an up-to-date picture: Older photos of you may be more flattering, but they can also be misleading, and using them can make others think you lack confidence (at best) or honesty (at worst).

Be relaxed and face the camera: Looking too stern when you are the vivacious sort, or forcing a grin when you are a naturally sober person, are bad moves. Just relax, be open and try to get an image that captures the real you in some way.

Collect pictures you like: When you see a picture you like of yourself (on a friend's Facebook page, for instance) download it (or scan it in if it is a hard copy) and keep it in your personal content folder.

Avatars

Avatars are representations of you in digital spaces. In 3D virtual worlds like Habbo Hotel (http://www.habbo.co.uk/) and Second Life (http://secondlife.com/), this means creating a virtual person to represent you in digital space. We won't get into that here – though the day may come when a 3D avatar will need to be part of your personal content library – we are more concerned with the much more commonly used 2D image avatar.

A standard corporate photo or publicity shot will be sufficient for LinkedIn, professional forums and the like, but what of everywhere else?

For the most part, use images that show your face. People want to know who you are: it's a very fast way for people to understand some basic information about you – your age, etc. We feel more comfortable when we know who we are speaking to.

---

[53] http://www.gimp.org/

Avatars can be a lot more playful. Some people choose cartoons, images they like or slogans as their avatars. Twitter users have taken to adapting theirs to be certain colours or to carry buttons and ribbons to promote various political causes or to promote a particular issue.

One service that I would recommend registering with is Gravatar (http://en.gravatar.com/). When you upload your photograph to make an avatar you can then use that image when you leave comments on blogs, for example. As you are not going to be sure where this image is going to crop up, it's probably best to use something you are comfortable with in both professional and social contexts.

If you want to play with your avatar image, there are hundreds of sites letting you create Simpsons, South Park or Mad Men cartoon versions of yourself or you can upload your own photos to the free avatar editing website, befunky.com, and create all sorts of interesting effects.

Biographies

Here's some advice for writing anything[54] that we may well come back to but which is especially appropriate when we have the awful job of writing wonderful things about ourselves:

- Who are you writing for? You are, basically, writing for people who don't know you. Depending on your industry or likely audience, you will need to adjust your style. Lawyers, bankers and other conservative professionals are unlikely to want to be overly chatty or effusive in their biographies (but it is entirely possible that I am being lawyerist in this regard, and mavericks exist in every profession, I am sure).
- Most people only read the first line and skim...: So get the important stuff in upfront and be as brief as possible. The rule for writing press releases and news stories is the same: write so that it can be cut paragraph by paragraph from the bottom and still make sense (if you do this you will also be able to write just one biography and cut it as required).

---

[54] Yes, please do feel free to apply these principles to everything.

- **How will the biography be used?** Your biography is unlikely to get you a job or win you a contract on its own. It is there, especially on websites, to do two things: first, help people identify you and quickly work out – along with scanning the rest of the information about you – whether it is likely to be useful for them to listen to you, talk to you or find out more. Second, if they have spent some time finding out more about you, they will want a quick way to explain who you are to other people.

- **Clichés are either invisible or painful:** We wear out language with over-use and misuse. Try out some phrases for size that may have once meant something but now mean nothing: 'leading solutions provider', 'leverage sales targets' and 'executive leadership responsibility', for example. They slip though the eyes into the brain and down into the 'forgotten already' pile in your cortex before you know it. Write out whatever you need to and then go back over it asking 'does that sound like something a real person would say?' and 'does that sound boring?' If the answer is yes, imagine yourself explaining the point to someone you like and trust, then write it out that way: matter of fact, plain speaking, honest English.

- **Think about what your 'one-sentence story':** Think objectively about what your story should be and whittle it down to a single sentence. Imagine someone who knows you professionally describing you to someone else they think should work with you. The trick here is to keep to the truth and avoid over-engineering the description: 'An award-winning pre-eminent practitioner of business development with five years' experience across several key sectors.' No one would say that – and if they did you wouldn't trust them. Again, defer to trusted friends on this one if need be, both for inspiration (how would they describe you to someone else) and sanity/vanity-checking of what you come up with. The one-sentence story can be the first sentence of your biography, or you can just keep it for reference while you write your biography.

- **Work out your key messages:** Similarly, you need to be clear on what the two or three things are that you want people to remember about you. These are stories too, in that they are little parcels of information about you that you want people to pass around. Begin by listing your skills, your experience and achievements and then pare these back to three to five statements that you most want people to remember.

Phone a friend?

As a last resort (or perhaps as a first one), get someone you can trust to be honest and who knows your potential audiences to take a cold, dispassionate look at your biography. Get them to write down their impressions as they read it and give you feedback. Take what they say on board.

If you suffer from intense biography-writer's block or a dread of writing about yourself, you could try swapping with a friend or colleague and writing one another's biographies.

'Word cloud' yourself

Another approach to writing an account of yourself can be to ask others what their impressions of you are. When he was applying for a big job a colleague of mine emailed everyone he had worked with and asked them to send him three words they would use to describe him (and begged them to be honest).

He compiled all the words into a list and created a word cloud, a visualisation where words are larger or smaller based on how often they are used.

You can create your own word clouds using a number of free online tools. One of the best is Wordle. Here is how to create your own word cloud:

- email close friends and colleagues and ask them to describe you or the person you are creating the word cloud for with three words;
- collate these words into a single document;
- go to http://wordle.net and click on the 'Create' menu at the top of the page;
- copy the words in your document, paste them into the box on the page, then press the 'Go' button.

Your Wordle word cloud will now be displayed. You can change the appearance using the menus just above the image.

Actually, Wordle word clouds are useful for all sorts of things. You can make them from the text in any document (take a look at the gallery on Wordle.net). Here for instance is the word cloud for this manuscript right at the moment that I am writing this sentence:

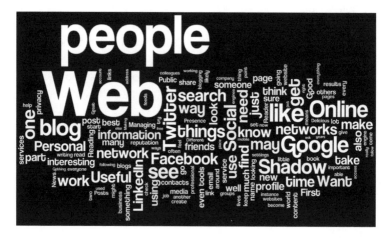

You can also get a word cloud for any website with an RSS feed (paste the web address into the second box on the 'Create' page on Wordle) or anyone's Delicious account.

CV and portfolio

A good place to start is to create or update your CV. Think of it less as a means of applying for jobs and more as the current state of your career.

Try starting the CV off with your one-sentence story as a summary and then create a document no longer than a couple of pages that lists achievements. Again, avoid the completist urge here – you don't need to include everything, you need to be informative and compelling enough to make the reader want to have another conversation with you to find out more.

Portfolios, a selection of past work, are stock-in-trade for people in creative industries. They are something everyone should consider having to enhance their web shadow, and as a personal resource.

How to create a personal portfolio

- Create a timeline of work: Count achievements as projects you have completed or contributed to.
- List, then make a précis your achievements, using your work timeline.
- Find images of work or that illustrate/represent projects you have worked on
- Create your portfolio: If you have a creative idea about how to present your work online, go for it. A basic, easy approach is to use Powerpoint (or Apple Keynote, or other presentation software). Insert your images as you see fit – your default preference should be having the images take up the whole of each slide's area with a simple caption on a white background text box. With your work in a slideshow format like this, you have a very versatile piece of personal content – you can post it to SlideShare (see Useful tools for managing your web shadow in Part III for more on this), as it is or with an audio commentary. Using SlideShare or other means you can also then display it on your personal website, blog, LinkedIn or other social network profiles and you can print it as a handout for clients, prospects or employers when you are going for a new job (or even a pay rise).

This approach can be useful to potential employers, colleagues and clients, but may have some value in its own right as an exercise in thinking about your achievements, the stories that you tell about yourself, the things you have to be proud of and should be communicating to others.

Some people like to have a CV website, or portfolio where they publish all this content. If you are a freelancer, sole trader or small business this is a great idea. If you are employed full-time already and aren't looking for a job, your LinkedIn profile will suffice, but it is a good idea to keep these documents up to date as a matter of personal due diligence: you are keeping your achievements on record, fresh and up to date and are ready to move when opportunity comes knocking, whether it is making a case for promotion or the job of your dreams suddenly comes up (or, er, both, obviously...).

We aren't all designers (even if we think we are)

A quick word about design. We all have access tools that can be used for design – even word processors, basic photo editors and presentation applications are more powerful than what a lot of professionals had access to a decade or so ago. Unfortunately we don't have access to the skills and taste that those designers have. Even more scarily, we sometimes think we do.

If you don't know a design professional, and most of us don't, then just keep CVs, portfolios and the like as simple as possible. If in doubt, use the most plain template that comes with your word processor or create a simple one using Helvetica typeface, plenty of white space and fonts no smaller than pt.11.

Hard copies – harder than you think to do well

All of your personal content can, of course, be used in the real world as needs be. Do make sure your home printer is up to the job of producing professional copies, otherwise make a trip to your local print shop. What looks superb on the screen can look like a pile of rubbish if it comes out faded and streaked from a basic printer running on half-empty cartridges.

3. useful tools for managing your web shadow

There are far too many useful services and websites out there for me to list comprehensively here. By the time these words meet paper and are shuttled out to a bookshop or Amazon distribution centre near you, there are likely to be even more.

As with so much in this book, the following constitute a very personal view of some of the most useful, mostly free, tools online to help you be aware of and make the most of your web shadow. Some of them are quite useful for a lot of other things too...

Getting connected

Let's begin with the nuts and bolts of being able to connect to the web in the first place. The art of managing your web shadow and your online life is all about removing barriers and things that slow you down. Get the fastest connection you can and a computer that has performance and portability in the right balance for the way you work.

- A personal machine: It may be that your main access to the web is via a work PC or laptop or that you share a computer at home. If you can afford it, get a laptop or netbook to call your own. If you are intent on developing your web literacy and building an online presence, this is an essential. Netbooks can be the cheapest and most convenient option, especially if you are a commuter or spend a lot of time travelling. If you want to – or are likely – to use photography, graphics or video at all, then spend as much as you can.
- A fast web connection: There's no way round this, the faster it is the more effortless using the web will be.
- Mobile broadband: It is a luxury, but mobile broadband access via a 3G dongle can be very useful if you travel a lot.
- Mobile devices: I've been struggling with 'smartphones' (phones that

can access the web and do other smart things) for years, but recently a couple have started to be very effective mobile computing devices. In the UK, the iPhone and BlackBerry® seem to be the most popular with hyper-connected people, my preference being for the former.

■ Storage and back-up: Like insurance, backing up your data is boring until you need it. Ensure that you have your personal content library and any valuable documents backed up to an external hard disk and the most crucial information stored online too (note: some people back up their most important data by emailing it to themselves on Gmail, which has an enormous upper limit for storage).

The latest, greatest browser of your choice

Surprisingly, many people struggle by using the web on very old browsers.

Making sure you have the latest version of a web browser can make a lot of difference to how fast websites load and therefore to the overall experience and efficiency of using the web. You can have as many browsers on your computer as you like, so try out a few and work out which fits in best with your workflow.

Firefox

Firefox is hugely popular among people who work on the web and is approaching 50 per cent of the web browsers used in the UK. It is an 'open source' browser which means that thousands of volunteers around the world work on improving it all the time. It is beloved by people who work on the web, not least because it has the largest number of 'plug-ins' (around 5,000 at the time of writing), which are services that can become part of your browser and do anything from giving you direct access to your Delicious bookmarks to translating foreign language websites. If you try out Firefox, be sure to ask technically-minded friends for recommendations and take a look at the Add-ons web page (https://addons.mozilla.org/en-US/firefox).

A useful browser plug-in

Google Toolbar

One useful plug-in I would recommend if you are using the Internet Explorer or Firefox browsers is 'Google Toolbar'. It adds a set of tools that can be useful for – among other things – 'crap detection' with two features that will tell you a little about the page you are looking at:

1. PageRank: This needs to be set up by clicking on the spanner icon on the right of the Google Toolbar, then the Tools page and then checking the PageRank box.
2. Clicking on the drop-down arrow by the PageRank bar will allow you to access a feature called 'backward links'. Click on this and it will give you a list of some of the people linking to these pages.

Internet Explorer

Microsoft is working hard to make its browser work well and its most recent version was well received by the tech community. If you have a PC, this will come pre-installed – just check you are using the latest version. (Go to http://www.microsoft.com/windows/internet-explorer/default.aspx and download the latest version.)

Safari

Safari is Apple's browser for the Mac and the latest versions are very fast indeed. There is also a Windows version, but opinions are mixed as to how well it works. There aren't as many plug-ins available for Safari, but as a basic browser it is very good indeed.

Chrome

Google launched its own browser in 2009 and it is well worth a try. It has fewer plug-ins available than Firefox, but has a reputation for being a fast, reliable browser. At the time of writing, it is only available for Windows, but a Mac version is promised soon.

Webmail account

Having sorted out access and a browser, now let's check our mail...

A webmail account is the centre of your web shadow management routine, so get yourself one if you don't have one already. Yahoo!, MSN, AOL and Apple (with its Mobile Me service) all offer personal webmail accounts. My preference is for Gmail, provided by Google. It's very versatile, consistently introduces new features which keep improving it and connects well with services like Google Docs (free browser-based word processing, spreadsheets and more), Google Reader (an excellent RSS reader, as we will discuss below) and other services. Like everything else I've mentioned bar Apple's Mobile Me, it is free.

Management hub for your online life

Your webmail account is very important as it will act as your hub for managing different web presences, a store for your passwords and where search engines alerts will arrive letting you know that someone, somewhere is talking about you (amongst other things).

If you work in a large corporate or government organisation (or indeed anywhere with an overzealous IT department, you may want to see if you can access your webmail there or not. It's not essential – you can always manage these things at home – but if you are blocked, you may want to think about getting a personal mobile device or a 3G connection for a personal netbook to be able to access the open web when you need to.

> **Note:** Many people say that you should have an email address which is connected to your personal website address, and they may be right. I think, though, that we will chalk that one up as an advanced web shadow building activity. Some services, notably Gmail, will allow you to use your Gmail account with another web domain, for instance your personal website or that of your business if needs be (mostly useful if you run a small business).

Google account

You may well have a Google account already if you have created a Gmail account, used Picasa, YouTube or any of Google's other services. If not, you will need one at minimum to create your Google profile.

Google provides a wide range of (mostly) free online services that you can access with your single login. The following are a selection which you may find useful in managing your web shadow and wider online life

Google Docs

Google Docs gives you basic word processing, spreadsheets and presentation software that work inside your web browser window. If you have a reliable connection to the web they are more than workable as an alternative to computer-based applications for everything but more elaborate documents.

You can also upload or cut and paste documents into these as a form of backup or use them to co-create or edit documents with others. Simply invite others to edit a document by clicking on the blue 'Share' tab on the right hand side and then 'Invite people' on the drop-down menu.

Google account health warning: There have been a number of scare stories in recent years where people have lost access to their Google accounts or had them suspended or hacked. As you can pretty much run an entire business through Google services these days, it is worth stressing the importance of backing up documents in more than one place and having contingency plans in place – as you would do with any other way of managing your IT infrastructure on a small or a grand scale. This goes for any information you store in 'the cloud' (bits of the web run by other people): you should always keep a backup on a 'local' disk, i.e. in your home or office.

Google Reader

Google Reader	
What is it?	• A web-based news reader service. Subscribe to news, blogs and other 'feeds' and when new articles or posts become available they are sent to your Google Reader account.
Where to get it	• www.google.com/reader
Benefits	**Immediate benefits:** • Massively more efficient way of reading news and blogs than visiting websites. **Emergent benefits:** • essential part of blogging workflow; • mobile application combined with desktop improves reading workflow; • develop a powerful, personalised media database for research and reference; • follow other people's reading lists or recommendations, share your recommended articles and publish your reading list.
Alternatives	• 'offline' news readers like NetNewsNow; • email applications like Microsoft Outlook and Apple Mail can also subscribe to RSS feeds, as can some browsers, like Safari, using its 'Live Bookmarks' feature.

Superpowered reading

If there were just one web tool that I could recommend to people to improve their reading for work and indeed any interests, it would be Google Reader. It is a part of my everyday web use every bit as much as email and search. Let's run through how to use it and some of the ways it can help manage your web shadow.

RSS feeds

You can ignore this definition if you like: unless you are interested in the technical elements, you can go quite happily about the business of using RSS feeds without ever understanding exactly what they are.

RSS (Really Simple Syndication) is a technology which lets your reader, such as Google Reader, know when new content is available from a website. In essence, by subscribing to an RSS feed the content comes to you rather than you having to go and check websites to see what has been added. For instance, if I subscribe to the BBC's business news feed, soon after a new story is published it will appear in my Google Reader (or whichever application I am using to subscribe with).

For more, check out the BBC's definition and descriptions here: http:// news.bbc.co.uk/1/hi/help/3223484.stm

Setting up

Setting up an account

Once you have a Google login, you can go to google.com/reader and start your Google Reader account. As you sign in, Google Reader will give you a number of posts to introduce you to the service, including a video tutorial, which is worth watching.

Subscribing to feeds

As soon as you have your account, visit some of the websites you read regularly and subscribe to their feeds. You can do this in a couple of ways. First, by clicking on the RSS symbol in the address bar of your browser which will either be the words 'RSS' or a variation on this logo:

If you click on the RSS symbol in most browsers (not Safari), it will take you to a page that will let you subscribe, using Google Reader, iGoogle or other options. Click on the menu by 'Subscribe to this feed using' and select 'Google' then click 'Subscribe now'. It will then ask you if you would like to add to your Google homepage or Google Reader. Select 'Google Reader' and you will see the feed in your Google Reader account:

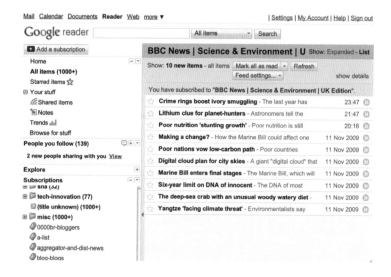

The alternative is to copy the address of the page you are in, then go to Google Reader and click the 'Add a subscription' button on the left hand side of the page. Then paste the address of the website into it.

Reading workflows

Pretty soon you will begin to accumulate a lot of feeds. You can organise these into folders easily, and as the folders act more like Delicious tags, a feed can sit in more than one. For instance, you can file the BBC business news feed under 'Morning reading' and 'Business'.

When you organise your feeds, one important thing to remember is that you have no limit on how much content is in your Google Reader account and it won't slow your machine down. All your feeds and their content live in the Google 'cloud' (its servers). Instead of deleting feeds for the sake of a more organised set of folders, you can create new ones and 'relegate' feeds to lower priority folders.

Folders can also be moved up and down by dragging and dropping them in your sidebar, so that the ones you want to view most often are at the top. My preferred system is to have:

- **Friends:** A folder for friends' feeds that I want to see whenever they publish things.
- **Priority reading:** The news and blog feeds so I can read all newly published material.
- **Bulk folder:** I keep the BBC, Mashable, some newspapers and a couple of other prolific professional bloggers in a folder of their own so that the quantity doesn't make me miss an important post from a friend or priority blogger.
- **Second-tier priority:** If I have time, I can read the second tier of blogs and feeds that I like. If not, they are all stored.
- **'River of news'[55] on my mobile:** I also like a bit of chance and randomness in what I'm reading, but I save this for when I am killing time on the move or just have a few moments to read something. You get this view of your feed by choosing to view 'All items' which will show all of the items in your feed reader with the most recent first.

Stars and mobile

One effective way of reading via Google Reader is to use the 'Star' function, especially when you are reading on a mobile device where you won't have a chance to do much with an interesting blog post or news article. Clicking on the star flags the item and you can view your 'Starred items' folder later on when you get back to your desk or somewhere you can do some work on your laptop.

This workflow has worked very well for me for sometime. Most of my reading on the move or while waiting for meetings to start is filtering my feeds to find useful articles I want to blog about, bookmark in Delicious or share with others. This means when I sit down with my computer to look at Google Reader I can immediately start reading and working on interesting and useful items.

Liking and sharing

Google Reader has many useful features to let you share items, manage your workflows more smoothly and to be useful to your network.

---

[55] 'River of news' is a phrase coined by writer, software developer and RSS pioneer, Dave Winer. His blog is at **http://www.scripting.com.**

- **Making connections:** There is a social network element to Google Reader which you can use passively by just letting it happen, or more actively by making connections and 'following' the Google Reader accounts of others. If you use Gtalk instant messaging, people you are 'Buddies' with and who have Google Reader accounts will automatically be connected to you on Google Reader. Everyone else you can manage through your contacts or by opting to follow them when you find their account in some other way (see *Like*, below).

- **Like:** If you click on the 'Like' icon under an item in Google Reader, it will show against the item for other users of Google Reader. It's kind of like a positive review or thumbs up at an individual article in the service. You can click on the '[number] people liked this link' and you will be given links to the Google Reader users who 'Liked' the piece. Exploring their profiles will show you other items they have shared, which can be an excellent way of finding new blogs and websites to subscribe to.

- **Share:** Clicking on the Share button will 'share' the item on your Public Page (see below) and be flagged to people who are connected with you to 'follow'.

- **Note in Reader:** There is also a 'Note in Reader' bookmark (available on the Sharing page), which you can drag to the bookmarks toolbar in your browser and use to share any page you see on the web via Google Reader. If you are using Delicious or another bookmarking function already, this would be doubling up on effort. How much effort you put into the sharing element of Google Reader is up to you – it can, in effect, become a social bookmarking network in its own right if you find that works well for you.

- **Email:** You can email a link to an item to someone you think will find it interesting or useful. Mailing links direct to people is a great way to be useful to your network, and a nice way to stay in touch with people and let them know you're thinking of them.

- **'Send to' bookmarks and other sharing:** You can bookmark to Delicious by opening the item you are reading (click on the blue headline and then bookmark as usual) or you can change the settings in Google Reader to do this direct from the item. (As with most workflows, this may only save a second or so, but it is the smoothness of not having to open new windows to do something new that can help you to keep your focus and work more effectively). To do this, click on the 'Settings' link in the upper right hand part of the screen, then choose the 'Send to' tab to the right hand of the screen, and choose the services you may want to bookmark or share items from Google Reader with, including Twitter, Facebook and Stumbleupon.

Public page

Google Reader accounts come with a public page by default. Take a look at this as soon as you have set up the account by clicking on the 'Shared items' link on the left of your screen. It shows details of your Google Profile and all the items that you have shared.

You can change your public page to be a little less public if you aren't comfortable with sharing too openly by clicking on the 'Sharing settings' link on the right hand side of the screen.

Subscribing to searches, and other useful feeds

RSS is an incredibly versatile piece of technology. All sorts of things are available, and you can subscribe to them in Google Reader and other news readers if you can think of reasons they will be useful to you. Here is a selection of uses I have found:

- **Searches:** You can subscribe to a Google Search Alerts (see *Exploring your web shadow (and beyond)* in Part II) and keep an eye on them all in Google Reader.
- **Bargain hunting:** Websites, like voucher codes, publish feeds of all the latest bargains.
- **Interesting people's bookmarks:** Delicious and other bookmarking services allow you to take feeds from all sorts of pages, including an individual's bookmarks, new posts around a particular tag and 'hot items'.
- **Forum threads:** If you come across an interesting forum thread, for instance (continuing on the theme of good deals) a discussion on

financial forum about a problem several people have in common with you about your bank's service – but you don't want to keep coming back to check on how the conversation is developing, you can subscribe to the feed instead.

■ Twitter: If you want to keep an especially close eye on what someone or a group of people are saying on Twitter, you can take it out of your Twitter application and into Google Reader. You can also follow someone's Twitter 'favorites' [US sp.] if they use that feature.

■ Flickr friends' photos: Grab a feed of a friend's photos, for instance if you want to follow their travels while they are on holiday.

Personal media search engine

Because you don't need to delete anything in Google Reader, it can effectively become a powerful personal media database. Having used Google Reader for some time, I have over 500 feeds, most of which I do not regularly read. So when I start a project where some research is required, I will often search first in my Google Reader for information. This personal search engine has proved very effective at giving me the latest thoughts and news from my network.

Sharing
Reading lists

Once your reading list is pretty good, you can share that too by creating a 'Reading List' (http://www.google.com/reader/view/#bundle-creator-page). It's one more way of being open, sharing and being useful to your network.

Connecting with others
Delicious (http://delicious.com)

What is it?	• A social bookmarking service.
Benefits:	• access to your bookmarks from any machine or your mobile; • no need to file, easy to retrieve and find things; • easy to share information with colleagues.

Emergent benefits:	• the longer you use it the larger a personal database of useful web content you have; • network features allow you to follow the reading/bookmarking activity of other users; • share your bookmarks to your blog or other web presences.
Alternatives	NB: Make sure that any social bookmarking service allows 'data portability' – i.e. you can move your bookmarks elsewhere or download them. After five years of saving things to Delicious, I would be devastated if I were no longer able to access my data. • Google Reader (http://google.com/reader). Features like being able to share to Google Reader mean that you can use it like Delicious, but it might be a bit fiddly. • Faves.com (http://faves.com/home) • If you find this a useful kind of service, Diigo (http://www.diigo.com/) is an advanced bookmarking and note-making system which is getting a lot of positive reports.

SlideShare (http://slideshare.net)

I love SlideShare and would happily write a whole chapter about it if there were space to do so. It's well worth checking out...

What is it?	• Allows you to upload and share your presentations (and other documents).
Benefits:	• easy to share presentations without sending big files over email; • lets you embed your presentation very easily into blog posts, your LinkedIn profile and other social networks.
Emergent benefits:	• synchronicity engine – puts your thinking/work out into the networks where all sorts of unexpected people may come across it; • stops wasted effort – gives your work a life beyond the workshop, conference or meeting it was created for; • a kind of social network in and of itself.
Alternatives	• Scribd (http://www.scribd.com) is a 'YouTube for documents' – very popular and offers many of the same features as SlideShare. • Google Docs (http://docs.google.com) is another useful way of sharing documents. It's more for collaboration, but will, for instance, let you share presentations on your LinkedIn profile.

Flickr

What is it?	• Photo sharing service. Free, with a premium option if you are uploading a lot of images.
Benefits:	• creates an online store of photographs, which is a nice backup/guard against computers getting lost or destroyed; • easy to share photographs with others, with simple privacy features.
Emergent benefits:	• sharing photographs under a Creative Commons licence can see your pictures end up being used in all sorts of interesting places (I've seen mine turn up in things like travel guides with a credit)*; • plugs into cool services like Moo.com that lets you have your photos printed on business cards and other things.
Alternatives	• Picasa (http://picasa.google.co.uk/): Google's online photo service.

* NB: if you are sharing photographs under creative commons, pick your licence carefully. You are giving away your creation, perhaps images of yourself and family. If you don't want them turning up in a company brochure or advert, for instance, choose a non-commercial licence.

Other tools

There are too many interesting tools out there to include every single one here, but these are some which you may find particularly useful.

Exploring and monitoring your web shadow

Site/service	Details	URL
Pipl	A 'people search' tool. Pretty fast way to get a snapshot of what your web shadow looks like and links to all sorts of other interesting databases.	http://pipl.com
Spokeo	Paid-for service. Markets itself rather salaciously: 'uncover personal photos, videos and secrets... guaranteed'. Searches through social networks to find information about a person. If you sign up it will also look through all of your contacts and find their information.	http://www.spokeo.com/
Blogpulse	A blog/social media search engine with trending visualisation tools. Useful if there is a lot of conversation about you for some reason.	http://blogpulse.com/

Socialmention	A great social media search engine that also provides rudimentary scores.	http://socialmention.com
Spezify	Another social media search engine, this one will present your results as a kind of collage of images and mentions in blogs and other websites.	http://spezify.com
Boardtracker	A specialist search engine for forums and messageboards.	http://boardtracker.com/
Icerocket	A social media search engine.	http://www.icerocket.com/

Establishing your web shadow presence/profiles

Site/service	Details	URL
Knowem	Checks if a username is free across lots of networks. Great if you are choosing a new alias (and also finding more social sites and services that you may never have heard of).	http://knowem.com/
Extendr	Paid-for personal presence website that aggregates all your feeds into one place.	http://www.extendr.com/
Domainr	Brilliant way to find web addresses that are available. For your name for instance...	http://domai.nr

Managing your web shadow

Site/service	Details	URL
Friendfeed	A personal aggregator that brings together in a single feed all of your activity on social networks, blogs and other places with lots of useful features like being able to create discussion 'rooms'.	http://friendfeed.com
Posterous	Posterous could be described as a blog you can email your posts or content to. It can also be a powerful tool for managing multiple presences on social networks.	http://posterous.com
Lifestream.fm	Another service that gathers feeds from all your web presences into one place.	http://lifestream.fm/

Ping.fm	You can post to multiple profiles from here, for instance sharing a status update between LinkedIn, Facebook and Twitter at the same time (you may not want to do this with *every* update). Allows you to use Instant Messenger and mobiles to post things as well	http://ping.fm/
Shozu	Update social networks or post content like photos to multiple social networks. Has some good applications available for some mobile phones too.	http://www.shozu.com/
Tumblr	A 'short form' blog with social networking features. Like Posterous, it can be an alternative to setting up a blog. Some cool features like automatically updating Twitter when you post.	http://www.tumblr.com/

RSS readers and home pages

Site/service	Details	URL
Bloglines	Free, web-based news reader, very similar to Google Reader and very popular too.	http://www.bloglines.com/
Pageflakes	Personalised homepage service like Netvibes. You can have blogs, news and anything else with an RSS feed.	http://www.pageflakes.com/
Netvibes	Same type of service as Pageflakes.	http://www.netvibes.com
iGoogle	Google's personalised homepage service.	http://www.google.com/ig
NewsGator (FeedDemon for Windows, NetNewsWire for Macs)	A computer-based news reader. Useful if you want to read your feeds when you aren't connected to the internet.	http://www.newsgator.com

Creating online groups and real-world events

Site/service	Details	URL
Ning	Ning lets you create a social network for anything for free. Some people use it to create big social networks, like Knit Picks, a knitting community with 18,000 members, or just a small, dedicated social network around an event like a conference or team away day.	http://www.ning.com/
Google Groups	A simple group communications tool. Particularly good for creating email newsgroups.	http://groups.google.com/
Yahoo! Groups	Similar to Google groups.	http://uk.groups.yahoo.com/
Wetpaint	Simple, free service to create wikis and social network-like communities. Charges extra for premium services.	http://www.wetpaint.com
Wikidot	Free for a basic service, monthly fees for larger ones.	http://www.wikidot.com
Upcoming	Lets you organise real-world meet-ups and events easily.	http://upcoming.yahoo.com/
Meetup	Like Upcoming, a really useful way to organise events.	http://www.meetup.com/
Facebook groups	As most people are members of Facebook, using the group function in Facebook can work well. You can also use this to promote events alongside Meetup or Upcoming.	http://www.facebook.com/

Further reading:

You could spend forever looking at all the wonderful, mostly free online tools out there. My personal rule of thumb is that if I can think of a tool or service that would improve some aspect of working on the web or managing my web shadow, then it probably exists already, so start Googling it...

Mashable, Makeuseof and ReadWriteWeb report on interesting tools and applications. You can also take a look at these choice compilations of online tools:

- J D Lasica: Coolest power tools of some top geeks: A great list of all the favourite tools and software used by a group of top geeks and bloggers: http://www.socialmedia.biz/2009/08/12/favorite-tools-of-some-top-geeks/
- Makeuseof.com: 20 tips to define and manage your social networks: http://www.makeuseof.com/tag/20-tips-to-manage-your-online-social-life-part-1/ and http://www.makeuseof.com/tag/20-tips-to-manage-your-online-social-life-%E2%80%93-part-2/
- The Social Text Participation Wiki http://socialmediatoday.com/SMC/106772

4. things you need to know about... LinkedIn

'CVs are boring! Honestly, once you've looked at 20 they all blend into one. Are they even necessary anymore, or would a LinkedIn page do the same job?'
Dirk Singer, founder of Cow PR[56]

Overview

Unless you are completely avoiding having a career, LinkedIn – as we have said a few times in this book – is one of the must-have parts of your web shadow. It is the public, professional part of your web shadow, something that is fast becoming as important as a CV.

One American survey[57] suggested that employers are more likely to check Facebook than LinkedIn when vetting potential employees. That may be the case, but if you have taken care of your privacy settings there, then LinkedIn is where they will end up. It is also likely that LinkedIn will feature prominently in search engine results for you.

LinkedIn is a social network for professionals, which claims to have more than 43 million members in 200 countries, and is still growing fast. People establish a profile with their professional experience and other details and connect to people they know or have worked with.

LinkedIn profile results tend to appear in Google searches for people's names these days and many people now use it as their first port of call when trying to find out about someone they may be working with, doing business with or when they are looking for candidates for a new job.

The simplest way to think of LinkedIn is as a 'live' CV. Approach setting it up as if you were preparing an application for your dream job – it really doesn't matter if you think you aren't going to change jobs in the foreseeable future, you still need your standing profile on LinkedIn to show you at your best. You might also think of LinkedIn as a permanent online

---

[56] http://www.thisisherd.com/2009/08/survey-says-pr-hires-must-be-up-on.html
[57] http://paidcontent.org/article/419-more-employers-scanning-facebook-for-new-hires-than-linkedin/

contact book: you can always stay in touch with people you have worked with or done business with no matter how many times you move job or lose your contact files or address book (if you still have one of those).

So, set aside some time to build and polish a proper profile on LinkedIn – you never know when you might need it.

In terms of who gets to see what information about you and thinking about privacy settings, let's be clear about how LinkedIn defines three different types of people online for you:

- My connections: People you connect to – you have invited them to be your contact on LinkedIn, like a friend on Facebook, or they have invited you and you've accepted.
- My network: Very broadly, anyone connected to people you know and, er, people they know. This is a lot of people: at the time of writing, there are 5.7 million people in my extended network in LinkedIn.
- Everyone: Anyone searching on Google or in the LinkedIn search system.

Setting up or re-setting your LinkedIn presence

First up, do you have a LinkedIn profile already? Even if you think you don't, do check by searching for yourself on the home page search bar (up in the top right hand corner). LinkedIn was founded back in 2002 and a surprising number of people have two profiles on the service as a result.

Two profiles can be confusing and look a bit unprofessional when people come looking for you, so rather than starting a new one, try to find a way to log in to the old one and start again.

When setting up your profile, you may want to register with your personal email address. Again, you may not be thinking about going for a new job at the moment, but if you were to it would be better if that mail were not going through your corporate email account for all sorts of (hopefully) obvious reasons. If you don't have a webmail, you will need to set one up. Yahoo!, Microsoft Hotmail and Google all offer services (my preference is for the latter).

Having a complete profile

LinkedIn encourages you to build a complete profile, and measures your progress towards achieving this with a little percentage status bar. It is worth getting this to 100 per cent in order to make your profile as useful as possible to people visiting it.

Let's walk through the elements of the profile – bearing in mind that some details of LinkedIn may have changed since I wrote this.

Basic information

Name: Use the formation of your name that you have decided to be consistent with online (see *Establishing your web presence* in Part II). You can choose to display only your first name and last initial if you wish, meaning that only contacts can see your full name. Unless you are in a 'small world' profession or have strong reasons or preferences for close security around your identity it's unlikely that this is a good option.

Professional headline: This is not your job title, although you might plump for exactly that and that alone if your job title really does clearly sum up what you are all about. Try to think of a broad, unpretentious, clear description of what you do professionally.

Country & postcode: Being clear about your location may help you find useful contacts near you.

Industry: Oddly, this can be a tough call. So you're a lawyer working in-house for a shipping company. Are you in 'Legal Services' or 'Maritime'? Don't worry about it too much – just plump for the one you feel most a part of (or maybe would like your next job to be in).

Photo: Photos add a lot to a profile. As discussed in the Personal Content section (see *About me: Creating and managing your personal content* in this section) find a good quality, recent picture of yourself to go in here. If you don't have one – get one. Again, you can choose who gets to see the photo from Connections, My Network and Everyone. Unless you have particular reasons for not letting anyone see what you look like, then 'Everyone' is the best option.

Public profile: LinkedIn gives you a lot of control and very clear settings over what other people can see about you on the web. You need to consider your preferences over privacy here, but my recommendation is to be open unless you have good reason to be more confidential. This being a professional social networking website, it's unlikely you will have a lot of sensitive personal information on display anyway.

Employment and education: As a rule of thumb, keep this information to what you would put on a CV. It's good to have a full employment history, but there's no need to provide every last detail.

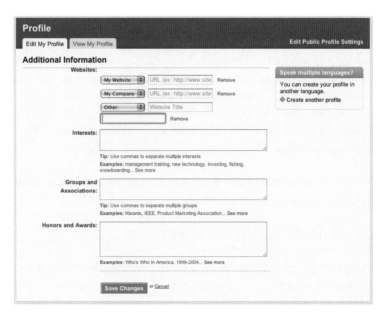

Summary: For some, the summary section will be the hardest section of all to complete. I worked in public relations and have drafted more executive biographies than I would care to remember, but still writing my own is something I find very challenging indeed. If you have read and completed the section 'Personal Content' then you may want to just paste in your biography – but do re-read it and tweak if you think it is a bit too pompous or formal for a social network. Remember colleagues and peers as well as the prospective employers will want to read it and be informed but not put off by it. Keep it real, as they say, but equally, don't be too modest or you will end up coming off as bland.

Interests: This is another section which people frequently struggle with when writing their CVs. Reading and going to the cinema are the defaults of shrinking violets, whilst extreme sports and golf feature large in the mythical CVs of the ultra-careerist. Err on the side of being honest and human, the purpose of these sorts of things is to show that you are.

Websites: LinkedIn allows you to list three websites on your profile – categories include 'My Website', 'My Company', 'My Blog', 'My RSS feed', 'My portfolio' and 'Other'. You need to select which three of these are going to be most useful for people. Prioritise your personal website/blog if you have established one of these – it will be the most useful resource for people wanting to find out more about your work. When linking to your company website think about linking to a section which is specifically about the area you work in. It's easy for someone to Google a company's name to find its home-page – the specific division or specialism you are working with may be harder to find.

Do use all three websites and make them link to pages that are about you, if possible. It strengthens your web shadow by making it easier for people to find out the good stuff about you and may well help make sure all that good stuff appears more prominently in search engine results for your name too.

Groups and Associations/Honors (sic) and Awards: Don't be shy now. If you have worked on projects that have had awards, make sure that they are listed here. Also make sure you list any industry bodies and other associations you are part of. This information gives a more rounded view of you to others and can help you make connections with others with similar interests. Take a look at the LinkedIn groups that are on the website – you may find some which correspond to your industry, your university or college, or to your personal or professional interests. If you join any of these they will be displayed as badges in your Groups and Associations section in your LinkedIn profile.

Personal information: Again, this is a personal privacy/security question as to how much personal information you want to share. My preference is not to store my personal information on LinkedIn, as I'm not sure how relevant it is to this network. Also, I am cautious of people using my contact information to spam me on email/IM or put my home address on direct mail lists. If people want to get in touch with me it is fairly straightforward to do so via LinkedIn or by visiting my blog or personal website. If I were working as a freelancer or contractor, however, I might want to make it as easy as possible for people to get in touch with me about potential jobs.

Thinking about a contact policy: There are two things to decide on when it comes to managing how people contact you on LinkedIn:

1. Are you happy for anyone to contact you via 'InMail', LinkedIn's closed email system or do you only want people to be able to contact you via your network? If you choose the latter then people will need to be a friend-of-a-friend in order to be able to mail you. Generally LinkedIn is pretty good at keeping spam out of its system, so the worst you will get if you allow anyone to contact you is a clumsy approach from a recruiter who has not read your profile properly. My recommendation is to allow anyone to contact you – you can always restrict this again if you are so intensely attractive to prospective employers that all those job offers get annoying.
2. The other setting is 'Opportunity Preferences' where you can publicly state what kind of opportunities you are interested in hearing about

from other people. Some people can feel awkward about ticking 'Job inquiries' or 'Career opportunities' when their boss might see them. The best policy to my mind is to tick all of them as a matter of course, in line with an 'open minded' policy. A legitimate response to snide remarks from colleagues about this is that you would be foolish not to want to know about the job market from a professional due diligence point of view (which competitors are hiring, what are the market rates). What sort of fool would declare themselves uninterested in that valuable information?

Building your contacts network

Once you have completed your profile, the next task is to connect with contacts and start building your LinkedIn network.

Who is a contact?

LinkedIn, rather presumptuously (in my view), has an automated email message to people you approach to become contacts 'Since you are someone I trust…'

But who should you include in your contacts? People you trust? What does that mean? People you have worked with closely enough to be able to vouch for their work? Most people I have spoken to adjust 'trust' to 'know' or 'don't distrust'.

Some people think of LinkedIn as a broader business contacts network, and include people they only know by reputation or from meeting online in networks like LinkedIn. Others are much more strict and limit it to people they know well. This places a higher value on their connecting to someone, but it also makes their world a little smaller. The opposite of this approach is people who think of LinkedIn as a 'numbers game' and work hard to get as many people to join their network as possible. Maybe this devalues their network a little, and gives an impression to some of an individual interested in scale over substance: networking for networking's sake.

To avoid dilemma-induced headaches, think of your own policy for agreeing to be people's contacts. You can reserve the right to change that policy later, of course.

Importing contacts

One of the easiest ways to get your contact network up and running is to import your contacts file from Outlook, Mac Address Book or any other contacts management software you might be using. This is a little bit fiddly, but basically involves exporting your contacts from your computer's address book and uploading them to LinkedIn. The LinkedIn website has plenty of advice on how to do this, but if you search for 'export' in your Outlook, Mac Address Book or other application it will tell you how to create a file.

Once the address book file is uploaded to LinkedIn (find the 'Import Contacts' tab in the 'Add Connections' section and click on the 'Other Address Book button') you can choose which contacts you would like to invite to become contacts in your network. Usefully, the details for the people that you don't invite remain available to you on LinkedIn.

As you can see, this process is a great way of backing up your address book. Even if your computer and your backup disks were destroyed you would always have your LinkedIn data next time you log on to the website. You can always download all this data again from LinkedIn (via the 'Export' feature in the 'Contacts' section).

You can also get LinkedIn to take your contacts out of your personal web-based email, like Gmail, Yahoo or Hotmail accounts. If, like most people, you have personal and work email accounts it is a good idea to run them all through LinkedIn.

Once it has your contacts data, LinkedIn will let you select which people you want to invite to become part of your network. Ticking checkboxes against their names means that they will be sent an automated message saying something along the lines of:

'I'd like to add you to my professional network on LinkedIn.'

If they accept you will get an email back to your web account.

Search

Use the LinkedIn search feature to look for people you know by name and also to revisit old companies or organisations that you have worked with.

Following the links

Another way to find people you want in your network is to follow the links to people in your contacts' networks and through Groups (see below). You are very likely to come across people you have met or worked with and not added to your address book.

Getting introduced

One nice feature, albeit one I have not seen used all that often, is the ability to ask someone in your network to introduce you to someone else. When you have found someone via search or in the contacts list of someone in your network you can ask to be introduced to them. Click on the 'Get introduced through a connection' link next to their profile and write a note saying why you want to connect. You can also put a separate note for the person you are asking to introduce you.

If someone asks you to introduce them to someone else, the default would be to always say 'yes' whenever you can, but to pause and think for a bit if for some reason you don't feel comfortable. If you are unsure or do not feel it would be appropriate, it would be best to reply to the person who is asking with a polite explanation of why you don't feel able to do this for them. They may have another way of getting in touch, so letting them know as soon as possible is the politest thing to do.

If the person you are try to connect to has a '3rd' symbol next to their name, it means that they are in the network of someone in your contacts' network. To get a message to them your note will need to be approved by your contact and then by their contact.

This happened to me once. Someone asked me to introduce them to someone two connections away from them, in the network of a client of mine, to whom he wanted to pitch a project idea. I did not pass on the message for two reasons: the client was a new one, and our relationship was not developed enough for me to ask this kind of favour. His contact was a senior peer in another country and I was worried it might seem like an imposition to introduce someone wanting to pitch to him. On reflection, I was maybe a little over-cautious, but you need to know someone at least a little before you start asking favours like this.

De-connecting?

LinkedIn is actually very helpful with this rather delicate matter and unless someone is looking out for this specifically they won't immediately notice if you un-friend them on LinkedIn. Given that LinkedIn is effectively a business contacts network, however, it's unlikely that you will want to 'un-friend' someone unless there is a serious reason you don't want to be seen to be connected with them.

Who's viewed my profile?

One quirky feature in LinkedIn is the 'Who's viewed my profile?' section. You will find the link to this down the right hand side of your home page, saying something like '10 people viewed your profile in the last 10 days, yesterday you appeared in search results 6 times'.

Clicking through, it doesn't give you a complete set of information about who has been looking at your profile, but teasingly gives you hints like 'Analyst at iCrossing' or 'Someone in the Art & Design function in the Online Media Industry from Manchester'. You can click on these intriguing descriptions and see a list of people from your extended network of contacts and contacts' contacts.

The 'Who's viewed' is a clever trick on the part of LinkedIn to show you that your profile is working for you, attracting attention. Try taking a look regularly if you are actively looking for a job and have been sending out your CV, applying for a job internally at your organisation or at other times when people might be looking to find out more about you. It is sometimes intriguing what you find out.

LinkedIn features

We have covered some of the features of LinkedIn in the previous chapter above, but here are the best of the rest...

InMail

LinkedIn describes InMail as a 'brokered communication channel through which you can send business and career opportunities to LinkedIn users'. What it means is that InMail is a way of getting in touch with people who aren't in your network of contacts that you would like to talk to but without letting you have their email address.

Most people have experienced it being used by recruiters wanting to get in touch with them as potential candidates. Unless you are a recruiter, researcher or sales professional it is unlikely that you will need to use InMail.

Recommendations/endorsements

LinkedIn users can give one another endorsements – in effect, short, public recommendations of their work.

It is best to reserve giving endorsements for people you have worked with or known well for a while.

Here are some pointers:

■ **Focus on their strengths:** You are not giving a full and comprehensive assessment of them as a person. If someone wants a full reference they will get in touch. Focus on the elements of their personality and work that were most impressive.

■ **Be honest:** Don't go overboard or make up positive things about them. They may be flattered but others may question your judgement and motives.

■ **Be concise:** A collection of brief positive endorsements looks great on a LinkedIn profile. People visiting will be forming an impression based on the spread of endorsements. So keep your comments to three or four sentences that convey your overall impression of the individual.

When an endorsement is given, the person receiving it can choose whether to display it or not. If an endorsement you are sent is lukewarm, you may not want to display it on your profile: 'X was a punctual and agreeable colleague' won't add a lot to someone's impression of you when they visit your LinkedIn page.

A last note on hierarchy: to avoid making people feel uncomfortable, avoid asking junior members of your team for an endorsement while they are still working for you (when they leave it is usually fine). It is often going to be problematic writing an honest, public endorsement of your boss. If they are honest and positive, they may be seen as obsequious, and if they are lukewarm they may be seen as critical. This is ultimately a matter of personal judgement, of course.

Status updates

Status updates in LinkedIn work just like the status updates in Facebook or a tool update. You enter a short text message (you can also post links) notionally in response to the question: 'What are you working on now?' People can comment on your status updates.

Some people want this status update to be the same as their Twitter and Facebook status and there are various tools and tricks that might help you do that – such as Ping.fm - but be wary of simply broadcasting everything to everyone – in the wrong context, like LinkedIn, these messages may begin to look like, feel like spam to other people in your networks.

As this is a social space about work, my preference is to update occasionally when you are working on something new and that may be of interest to your wider network, or add a link to something online that you are proud of (news coverage, an event, a video of a presentation or similar). It might also be good to post status updates if you are actively looking for a new project or job (if you don't mind your employer knowing about it), or if you are hiring or looking for collaborators.

Try to avoid updating automatically to this from your blog, or if you do, keep an eye on what is getting posted. Perhaps ask some other people in your network what they think of your status updates – the last thing you want to be doing is spamming your networks.

Premium service option

LinkedIn is free to all, but it does offer various premium options. They give the user the ability to send InMail messages to people they aren't connected to, see more profiles when they search and set up search alerts which tell them when people create or update profiles that might be of interest to them (for instance if they have specific skills that they want in a candidate for a job).

If you are a recruiter, business development professional or researcher of some kind this is very useful indeed. Most people though, will never need access to the premium services of LinkedIn and they certainly are not essential to managing your web shadow.

Groups

There are thousands of groups on LinkedIn that you may find it interesting or useful to join. They tend to be set up around professions, industry or expertise areas and organisations, but you can set up just about anything you like.

Many events, such as conferences, will start a LinkedIn Group by way of extending the life of the show and helping attendees to keep in touch with one another.

Have a look and see whether your school, university and previous employers are there along with any professional organisations you belong to. Some people join groups and are rarely active in them, acting as latent parts of their networks and badges on their profiles – part of their public identity.

The most interesting groups are likely to be ones which are organised around things you are interested in at the moment. To get the most out of these try to visit them regularly and find discussions you can join. When you visit the Groups section of your LinkedIn page you can reorder your list of groups so that the ones you're participating in most actively are at the top of your list.

It is also easy to start a group yourself on LinkedIn by clicking on the 'Create a Group' button on the Groups page.

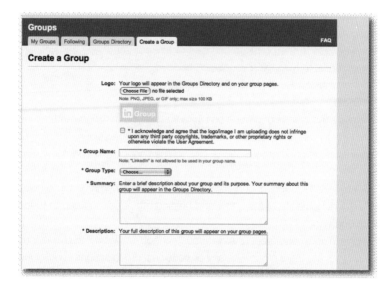

Answers

In LinkedIn Answers, people can ask or answer questions. People can also review questions within their Groups and contact networks (extending out to your contacts' contacts and even their contacts). Questions are asked within categories and sub-categories.

As part of exploring LinkedIn and in the spirit of being useful, take a look through your area – or areas – of expertise and see what people are saying and whether you can answer any questions. Some people choose to be useful to their networks by spending time regularly answering the questions of others.

When you ask a question on LinkedIn it is posted in public for anyone to respond to within seven days, although you can 'close' the question at any point. When you do close the question you will be asked to select which answers are 'Good' with a tick in the checkbox. If you select just one answer that becomes the 'Best Answer' – which people will see first if they review the Q&A later. The individual who gives the 'Best Answer' has that achievement added to their profile.

In my network at the moment, someone called Daniel has the highest Best Answer scores and he gets his accomplishments proudly displayed on his public profile like this:

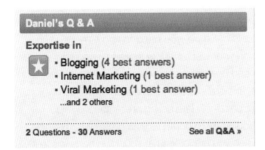

It is not uncommon to see people promoting their products or services as part of their responses. Often this is legitimate, but in the spirit of being useful, it is best to do this sparingly and only where talking about what you can sell to people is really the best way to add to the conversation.

So, a nice way of being useful, potentially making new contacts and showing that you really do know what you are talking about.

Applications

LinkedIn applications are web-based services that you can plug in to your profile to add some colour and make it more useful or help you connect with other people in your network.

It is likely that a good few new applications will be added between the time of my writing this and the book finding its way to you, but here are a selection of my favourite applications and why they may be useful to you:

Amazon Reading List
- **What the application does:** Shows what you are reading and what people in your network are reading at the moment.
- **Why it is useful:** If you know someone who is interested in the same things as you and that you admire, knowing what they are reading is a

great way to understand more abut their perspective. This application is naturally also superb for finding what books to read next.

SlideShare

- What the application does: Connects with your SlideShare account (if you don't know about SlideShare, you need to know more – see *Useful tools for managing your web shadow* in Part III) and showcases your latest documents and presentations on your LinkedIn profile.
- Why it is useful: Again, this is a share-and-discover application which will get attention for your dazzlingly interesting presentations and documents as well as adding more depth to your profile when people come to take a look. When you are looking at your own home page it will show you highlights from your network's SlideShare accounts – another way of finding out about what people are doing and thinking about.

Wordpress

- What the application does: Connects your Wordpress-hosted blog (See *Useful tools for managing your web shadow* for blogging tips) with your LinkedIn profile. People visiting your profile will see that you have a blog and links to recent articles.
- Why it is useful: Blog Link is also available if you host your blog on the Typepad, Blogger, LiveJournal or indeed the Wordpress platform.

TripIt

- What the application does: Connects you to the Tripit service which lets your contacts know when and where you are travelling.
- Why it is useful: If you travel a lot in your job, this service or Dopplr, can be helpful in letting you know when people in your network are going to be in the same city at the same time, kind of acting as a top-level public diary. Note: Be very careful if you set up a TripIt account however when it comes to inviting contacts. A clumsy slip of the mouse made me into a spammer as all of my Gmail contacts were hit with invitations to join the service.

5. things you need to know about... Facebook

Facebook and your web shadow

Even in the context of the huge numbers which characterise success on the web, Facebook is a giant. At the time of writing, Facebook has grown to more than 250 million active members around the world. By the time this book is published I would expect to see that number in excess of 350 million or more.

As well as attracting huge numbers of users, Facebook is notable for the way it has taken social networking, an activity previously seen as the preserve of geeks and teens, and brought it emphatically into the mainstream.

Every two years, the Oxford Internet Survey (OxIS) takes a look at how people in the UK are using online communications and media. In 2007, it first registered 'social networking' as a distinct type of online activity emerging – 17 per cent of British internet users at that time said they were using social networks. By 2009, in no small part to Facebook, almost half (49 per cent) of everyone online in the UK were on social networks.

Depending on who you listen to, Facebook is either a fad or is bedding itself in to become a permanent, defining feature of the social web. Frankly, who knows, but it seems likely that it will be an important part of many people's lives for some years to come. So Facebook requires close attention from people who want to understand and manage their web shadows for the following reasons:

- **People will look for you there:** Employers, friends, business contacts and colleagues are likely to use it if they want to find you, or find out more about you.
- **Risk management:** Facebook is so widely used in the UK and other countries that you need to be aware of how your reputation can be affected by content and conversation on its pages.
- **It is a useful platform:** Many people maintain a profile for their businesses, communities, clubs or events in Facebook. It can be the sole point for simple web presences or an important outpost of one that lives elsewhere on the web.

■ Connecting and distribution: If you are creating blog posts, videos or documents and slideshows elsewhere online, sharing them with your network on Facebook is another opportunity to let people know about interesting things that you are doing.

What's Facebook for?

It is likely that you already have a Facebook account. How, or if, you use it is another thing altogether. Sometimes people set up on Facebook, tinker a little and then wander off, slightly confused and bored. Others will go through a honeymoon period of utter infatuation, updating every few hours, enjoying the thrill of re-connecting with old friends and colleagues.

After our first encounters with Facebook, though, we need to decide why we are using it and how we are going to manage our interactions with it.

For many people, myself included, Facebook is developing into a very personal space, chiefly for communicating with people you know well, friends and family mainly, and sharing things like photos and amusing or useful bits of web content with them.

Facebook seems to be the frontline in the cultural negotiation our society is engaged in about where the line between our public and private selves online lies, and how our web shadow connects with our everyday lives.

Getting set up

As I mentioned, it is very likely indeed that you already have a Facebook profile, so I am not going to include a detailed walkthrough here. If you do need information about setting up, take a look at the official Facebook advice (http://www.facebook.com/help/new_user_guide.php).

Make sure that you complete your profile. Bear in mind that your profile photo is one of the few things that most people will see, even if you restrict access with your privacy settings, so go for something that you're happy for the world to see and that helps people recognise that it is you that they have found.

If you set up a while ago, it is worth taking a look through the different elements of your profile to make sure you are still happy with what is in there.

Your Facebook username

Facebook lets you set a web address for yourself. Give preference to your actual name, or variations on it, as this will make it easier for people to find you, or opt for an alias or nickname that you are using across your web shadow.

Your Facebook page

Facebook updates its look and feel fairly often, but most of the elements below will probably still apply. Take a look at Facebook's home page tour (http://www.facebook.com/sitetour/homepage_tour.php) if you need a more up-to-date view of how the service works.

Newsfeed/Stream

The centre column on your Facebook page has a stream of content, including wall posts, status updates, photographs and things people who are part of your network have 'Liked' or commented on. If you see an item that you think is interesting, you can 'Like' it by clicking on the button below it, and also leave a comment about it which will appear in the stream of the person who originally posted it. Other people among your friends and their friends will also see it (depending on your privacy settings).

You can change what you see in your stream in two ways. If you hover your mouse to the right of a post a button marked 'Hide' will appear. Clicking on this you can choose to 'Hide' the person who posted it, which means you won't see any more updates from them in your stream (they aren't notified about this, so don't worry about offending them).

The other way to change what you can see is to use...

Filters

The filters on the left-hand side of the Facebook page let you control what you are seeing in your main newsfeed/stream, selecting to see by Friends groups, if you have set these up, or types of content (like photos or videos).

Publisher

The publisher is the box that sits just above your news feed. You can use this to post a status update (a short message about what you are doing, thinking or anything you fancy) or links to content like YouTube videos, blog posts and pictures.

Click on the icons underneath the publisher's white box to do things like upload videos, music or create an Event, which you can invite people to.

If you are building your Facebook network or spending some time learning how it works then don't forget to post regularly, at least once a day. Some people link their Twitter account to Facebook, but this isn't to everyone's taste. See what works for you and your network of friends. My preference is to treat Twitter and Facebook as separate networks – I share only some things in Facebook that I would put out on Twitter and vice versa.

Requests

It's worth keeping an eye on the Requests box in the upper right-hand corner of your home page. You can see there if you have people asking to become your friend, inviting you to events or suggesting applications and web pages you may like.

Highlights

If you have a lot of Friends, or your Friends are making a lot of updates to Facebook, chances are you won't see everything. Facebook tries to guess what you will be interested in and posts some suggestions here.

Applications

There are thousands of free applications available on Facebook that you may find useful or entertaining. Two notes of caution when using these:

- **Be careful when inviting others to join you.** Some applications encourage you to invite all of your Friends. Think before you let them do this: are *all* my Friends really going to be interested in taking a personality quiz? Many Facebook users bemoan the frequent invitations they get to play games and take part in competitions from people they hardly know. It feels like spam to them and it makes you look bad.
- **Be aware of privacy issues.** When you use an application you allow its owner (usually a third party company, rather than Facebook itself) access

to your data. Most companies will only want to use certain parts of your Facebook data, like your name, profile photo and some details to help the application work. However, you need to be aware that your personal data is being shared, and that you won't necessarily be sure with whom.

Organising your Friends

Organising Friends into groups helps make sure that you are sharing the right kinds of things with the right people. For instance, close friends and family are likely to be interested in seeing pictures of my recent trip to the beach with my children. My preference is not to inflict these on my professional network or people I don't know very well.

You can organise Friends into as many groups as you like. Personally I keep my network to three groups:

- Friends and family: People I know very well and my family members.
- Professional: People I know well, but have an exclusively working relationship with.
- Acquaintances: People who I have connected with on Facebook only, or have met only once.

Privacy and Facebook

Note: Facebook changes its privacy settings and policies often. Please check www.antonymayfield.com/webshadows for the latest information and guides on Facebook and privacy.

In 2009, the newly appointed head of the British intelligence organisation, MI6, had personal information and photographs of his family and friends published in newspapers in a story which quickly spread around the world.

His wife's Facebook account was the primary source for this story. While she may have thought she was in a private social space, her profile was completely open to anyone who was part of the London network on Facebook (about 4 million people at the time).

The story, while hugely embarrassing for the people involved and the UK government, served to illustrate some important things about our online lives. First, such was the creeping, unnoticed spread of Facebook's version of web openness that even in parts of the establishment where privacy and security was most guarded, people had not thought to check the web shadows of the UK's top spy. If he was unaware of how Facebook privacy worked, what hope for the rest of us?

Many of us have heard horror stories of young people having college party antics posted on Facebook, or making stupid updates about how much they hate work and getting fired. Behind the salacious tales in the media, though, there are hundreds of embarrassments, small and large that happen on Facebook.

Understanding how privacy works on Facebook is a crucial piece of managing your web shadow. Due to the platform's popularity and its role as many people's first experience of the social web, of being able to publish thoughts, images and video to the web, or to take part in or run communities.

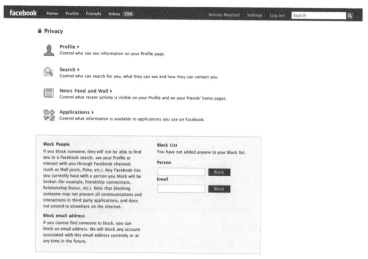

Settings

Finding the privacy settings

You can find your settings by clicking on the 'Settings' menu in the top right hand part of the screen.

Elements you can share

Hopefully, Facebook will develop simpler ways to manage your privacy settings – there is a growing demand from users for them to do so. Meantime, you need to know what the different parts of your profile are called and what sharing them with people will mean.

What Facebook calls it	What it includes
Basic info	Networks you belong to Gender Birthday Relationship status Political views
Personal info	Activities Interests Favourite music Favourite TV programmes Favourite films Favourite books Favourite quotations
Status and links	What you enter in your status window Links you post to your profile
Photos tagged of you	Any photos that someone tags (says is you)
Videos tagged of you	As with photos
Friends	Who you are Friends with
Wall posts	Anything people post on your wall
Education info	Whatever you have included in this area
Work info	Information you provide about where you work
Contact info	Whatever contact information you have decided to include. (I don't include any – people can email via Facebook if they need to get in touch.)
Pages	Things you are a fan of...
Groups	You can join Groups if you have installed the Groups application

Who can see what?

Now you're clear on the types of content you may want to control people's access to, you can decide who gets to see which bits of your profile, your status and other things that you would like to share.

You might find it useful to plan this in advance, before opening up the Facebook settings panel, as there will be some fiddling with sections and knowing who you want to see what will help you through it quicker.

This is an example of how you might sketch it out...

List	Include	What they can see
Friends & family	Close friends, family members.	Everything.
Professional	People I work or have worked with but would not socialise with at non-work events.	All my profile information and status updates, but not photos tagged of me, wall updates, or photos I upload.
Acquaintances	People I have met online or offline but don't know well.	All my profile information.
Limited profile	People you want to have little access to your information – just the basics.	My basic information only.
Networks	Anyone who is a member of the same networks as you – e.g. the place you live or your university.	Nothing. Personally I don't see a lot of value for me in these, though it may very well be different for you, especially with smaller networks, say you are at a college or live in a small village.
Everyone	Anyone who cares to look.	How transparent do you want to be? I lock down everything except my basic personal details.

Managing other people's privacy risks

When thinking about managing your web shadow in Facebook you can come face to face with what living in networks really means. While you can be careful about what you share and who can see it from your profile and the content you share, your privacy is only as strong as the other people in your network.

Take these examples...

...mentioning that you've won a major deal to your mum. It's still confidential but she's so proud she posts a congratulatory note on your wall. The new client who recently became a friend on Facebook sees it and has a melt-down as they haven't finished with the negotiation or told competitors that they have lost out.

...you go for a job interview at a competitor's offices. A friend who works there posts, 'Great to see you today – best of luck!' on your wall. A colleague tips off your boss and difficult conversations ensue.

You see what I mean. You don't need to be photographed in a compromising situation for someone to cause you problems due to their lack of understanding about how Facebook works.

Here are some points that can help you help others in this regard (thereby making yourself more secure):

- share a how-to guide to privacy on your Facebook profile and send it to friends, especially those closest to you (and more likely to mention personal information or post images);
- offer to walk through the setting up of privacy settings on their Facebook profiles for family members, colleagues and close friends;
- politely (usually privately) remind people who post sensitive information about you that it could cause you problems and why.

Further reading

- All Facebook: 10 Privacy Settings Every Facebook User Should Know: http://www.allfacebook.com/2009/02/facebook-privacy/
- How to use Facebook Privacy Settings, by ConnectSafely.org http://bit.ly/48gfwv
- Facebook privacy best practices for Facebook from security firm, Sophos: http://www.sophos.com/security/best-practice/facebook.html
- WIRED: Your Facebook Profile Makes Marketers' Dreams Come True: http://bit.ly/ZNf6L
- eHow – How to get started on Facebook: http://www.ehow.com/how_4581117_started-facebook.html
- Facebook's own guide to getting started: http://www.facebook.com/help/new_user_guide.php

6. things you need to know about... Twitter

What is Twitter?

> Note: Twitter's features are often updated by the company, check www.antonymayfield.com/webshadows for the latest information on Twitter updates.

At the time of writing – Autumn 2009 – Twitter may well be at the very peak of its hype bubble. However, whatever the mood at the time you are reading this chapter, take a look at Twitter.

Those in the technology trade refer to Twitter as a micro-blogging platform, but it works very differently to blogging. To a new user, it feels a bit like instant messaging, a more personal communications medium. To some it feels a bit like broadcasting text messages to the world. In truth, Twitter is very different to both of these things – it imports analogies, that don't tell us the whole story.

Twitter lets people publish very short – 140 characters – bits of text on the web, known as 'Tweets'. Each one of these can be seen on their Twitter stream, and can be read by anyone who visits their page or who 'Follows' them from their own Twitter stream.

Unless you keep your Twitter profile private, everyone can see every message that is posted and they'll even appear in search engine results and Google Alerts for keywords that you have set up.

Twitter in the wild – how it is used

Laura Fitton[58], a consultant who specialises in advising companies on social media and Twitter in particular, said: 'Something we are learning very fast is that Twitter makes a great command line interface...'.

---

[58] Laura is @pistachio on Twitter. She's also the co-author of *Twitter for Dummies*. http://books.google.com/books?id=r7XcxArlFgoC&printsec=frontcover#v=onepage&q=&f=false

That's a very geeky way of saying that Twitter is so simple that people are using it to do all sorts of things, from sharing photographs (e.g. TwitPic) to running polls (StrawPoll) and to-do list applications (e.g. Remember the Milk)[59]. Because Twitter's founders built it with openness as a key principle, people have created thousands of tools and services that both make the core Twitter service more useful and apply it in all sorts of unexpected ways.

The service has also evolved by listening to and watching the behaviours of its users. Many of its features – like using the '@' symbol to signify that you are addressing another user publicly – have been adopted and improved because people using the service have started doing that *en masse*.

Twitter is used in all sorts of ways then. Let's take a look at some of them:

- Social networking: First of all, people use Twitter as personal and public social networks. People follow and are followed by people they know, work with, or just find interesting.
- Distribution: A lot of newspapers and media organisations (@ GuardianNews, @bbc) maintain a Twitter presence to publicise their articles.
- Information services: Airports (@man_airport), clubs (@ cambridgeunion), music and sporting events (@glastofest) are using Twitter to keep people up to date with information. These sorts of feeds are usually useful for short periods, so people follow and un-follow them as needs be.
- News: If there is a big breaking news story, you can be sure that journalists and other Twitter users will be watching for eye-witness and expert commentary on what is happening. We saw this dramatically in 2009 when the first images of the Hudson River air crash came from a Twitter user on one of the ferries that went to the aid of passengers[60].

---

[59] Links to all of these examples and 96 other 'essential Twitter tools' can be found in this Smashing Magazine blog post http://www.smashingmagazine.com/2009/03/17/99-essential-twitter-tools-and-applications/

[60] Telegraph.co.uk: *New York Plane Crash: Twitter breaks the news, again* http://www.telegraph.co.uk/technology/twitter/4269765/New-York-plane-crash-Twitter-breaks-the-news-again.html

In the unrest following the Iranian elections in the same year, Twitter gave the world a street-level insight into what was happening, despite the government there putting strict controls on the media[61].

■ **Co-ordination:** People use Twitter as one tool to help them coordinate flash-mobs[62], and other events, even just simple meet-ups (sometimes, called 'Tweet-ups' of people who are friends on Twitter.

■ **Marketing and customer service:** Marketers are fascinated by Twitter's potential. Some do interesting things, others publish feeds of news and special offers (@marksandspencer) or a mix of information and advice (@bestbuy in the US is a great example of this).

■ **Games:** Some people see Twitter itself as a kind of game, scoring by how often they get re-tweeted, how many people follow them etc. But there are also games that use Twitter or are played out on Twitter (@ freemafiagame), although these can be deeply annoying to some users.

■ **Creativity:** There are a good few poets, writers and comics trying out Twitter's constrained space to enhance their creativity – 140novel was one such experiment that ended in early 2009, while TwiHaku pulls together haiku-like poems written in a single Tweet[63]. One popular project was a group of fans of the HBO TV series 'Mad Men' who tweeted as characters from the show, bizarrely blending 1960s lives and series plot-lines with 21st century web communications[64].

Twitter literacy

'I don't want to know what people had for breakfast!' is a frequent refrain from people who had opened up the site and found a stream of what looks to them very much like inane, irrelevant nonsense.

---

[61] BBC News, the Editors blog: Social Media in Iran http://www.bbc.co.uk/blogs/ theeditors/2009/06/social_media_in_iran.html

[62] http://en.wikipedia.org/wiki/Flash_mobs

[63] http://www.makeliterature.com/twihaiku/twitter-poetry

[64] The show's producers initially reacted unfavourably to this Twitter example of 'fan fiction' http:// www.businessinsider.com/2008/8/amc-to-twitterers-please-don-t-market-madmen-for-us

Twitter may not be for everyone, but that initial reaction should be tempered with an understanding that Twitter is something you need to take time to learn. The simplicity of Twitter sometimes makes it paradoxically difficult for people to understand it.

For readers of this book, using Twitter is definitely a 'Building' activity for managing your web shadow, but once you have decided to try it, think of it as a project, a new skill, or set of skills, to be learned. Toe-dipping is not the best approach for Twitter, I fear.

Think of it like learning to drive or play an instrument. You will know enough after a few hours to move the vehicle tentatively or string a halting tune. Give it 40 hours and you will be able to pass a driving test or play a passable song or two. When you hit 100 hours, you're going to be pretty confident and able to hold your own.

Perhaps think about logging 15 Twitter hours over the next couple of months (an hour a day every other day for a few working weeks, or two hours a day for a full week) to see if it starts to make sense. Then commit to a more regular schedule for a couple of months more to start learning it enough to be proficient.

Setting up your Twitter presence

Once you are set up with your Twitter profile, go into the 'Settings' (up in the right hand corner of your homepage).

Username and real name: Find a username that you like, or that matches approximately with your preferred 'handle' online. Be sure to include your fuller name as well.

Time zone: If you travel across time zones you can change this as you go – myself, I rarely remember to. Set it to home and don't give it any further thought.

More info URL: Even if you don't have a homepage, make sure you put a URL in here (LinkedIn or Facebook URLs, or a company biography page will do). As well as helping you connect up the different parts of your web shadow (helpful to others and to search engines, many people like to know a little more about someone before they follow them on Twitter.

One Line Bio: Twitter is a (very) public place; be clear on your personal/professional policy. If you identify yourself with your company, best to bear in mind that you may be held to account by them for anything you say.

Private or public: If you like, you can keep your Twitter profile locked down and private. Only people that you approve will be able to follow you and search engines won't be able to index what you have written so that other people won't see it when they search on a given topic.

Devices: In some countries, with certain carriers, you can send and receive Twitter messages by text message. As I have a web browser on my phone, I don't bother with this approach but some people find it very useful. Check if any costs are involved with your carrier before you throw yourself into this way of Tweeting.

Notices: Make sure that you keep the options ticked here to receive email notifications for direct messages (see below) and when you get new followers.

Picture: Make sure that you upload a picture to Twitter. You can start with a standard image, but lots of Twitter users like to adapt and play with their images.

Tip: if you want an interesting avatar you could do worse than visit http://www.befunky.com/photoApps.php# to turn your profile picture into something really special.

Design: Twitter gives you a set of themes you can put up on your Twitter profile, or you can upload your own image. Many people opt for a favourite photograph or something that reflects their personality. Hardcore networkers and people who use their Twitter profile primarily for business, or as part of their business web presence, include things like contact details and their other web addresses in a customised image. If you want to go the latter route, some companies offer a service creating Twitter backgrounds or if you're prepared to roll up your sleeves and use some image editing software take a look at this useful blog post on Mashable: http://mashable.com/2009/05/23/twitter-backgrounds/

Connections: This section shows you what other services you have connected up to your Twitter feed – for instance personal aggregators like FriendFeed (see *Useful tools for managing your web shadow*).

Getting your Twitter network started

First up you need to be following a healthy number of people so that you find interesting things in your Twitter feed when you go to check it. Clicking on the 'Find People' feature at the top of the Twitter home page will give you a number of ways of doing this:

- Find on Twitter: Searching for the names of people you know can take you direct to their profile. Then just click on the Follow button next to their name.
- Find them on other networks: Twitter will check your Gmail, Yahoo or AOL webmail account to see if anyone you know has registered a Twitter account.
- Invite by email: Just email people you know direct and invite them to join you on Twitter.
- Suggested users: Twitter recommends a load of top feeds, from big brands like Dell and newspapers like *The Guardian* that have feeds to some of the most interesting and followed Twitterers around.

Once you have got some people to follow, start listening. You will see them having interesting conversations, and Re-Tweeting (see below) what others are saying. Follow the @links and look at who the best people are following to find more people to follow.

Everyone has their own preferences about how many people to follow. At first I tried keeping my numbers down. I was treating it as a close, personal network. Over time however, I found it more and more useful to include a broader range.

For starters, I would try out 50-100 feeds and see how you go. If you find some are uninteresting or even irritating, you can un-follow them. Don't worry about watching the number too closely, it will creep up over time, but as long as you are finding the service still works for you, there is no need to conduct mass culls of followers.

Many of the tools you can use on Twitter (see below) allow you to create groups. For instance categorising people by 'friends', 'colleagues', 'news' and 'top feeds' works for me. I can view the type of Tweets I want at a specific moment, making sure that I don't miss Tweets from my closest friends, but then also just enjoy the serendipity and pleasure of browsing that comes from looking through the main stream of Tweets from the several hundred interesting people and organisations that I follow.

As ever, you need to try a few different approaches and let your own preferences and style of using Twitter emerge as you get to know your way around.

Being followed

Sooner rather than later, if you are following others and joining in the conversation you will begin to get followers. At some point you will begin to get email notices telling you that people you don't know are following you.

Follow the link to their profile and take a look. The biography, their linked-to website and their recent Tweets should give you a pretty good idea of whether you are going to be interested in following them. If in doubt, follow them back anyway – if their Tweets prove not to add much to your Twitter reading, you can always un-follow.

You will find that you attract some strange followers at times and some seem to be pushing services you would rather not hear about – business coaching, pharmaceuticals and dating services seem to crop up a lot for me – or seem to just be posting links to special offers. These are spammers. You can make sure they are not able to follow you if you press the button marked BLOCK.

Sometimes you will be followed by brands or organisations if you have mentioned them or something related to your products (a colleague of mine was followed by a tissues brand after he'd mentioned he had a cold, for instance!). As with people, whether you follow them or not is up to you and whether you think they will add much to your reading and Twitter experience overall. You leave them following you if you see no harm in it or, if you don't like them or the way they are acting, you can BLOCK them from your Twitter feed.

Unfollowing

Un-following someone on Twitter is as easy as following them – it's a click of button when you are visiting their profile page or viewing it in your Twitter application. People are not told by Twitter when you do this, but they may notice or be notified by a service they have running.

As we have noted before, some people will take it personally if you un-follow them, but it is best to keep the people you are following to those who are interesting and/or useful to you or using Twitter can become a drag. It is also best to have a thick skin and not take it personally if someone un-follows you. It's as likely that they are trying out different ways to manage the feeds they read or are just trying to slim down their follower counts.

Using Twitter

Using Twitter is as simple as writing out your 140-character Tweet and pressing 'Update'. Try saying a simple 'hello' or post a link to something interesting you have read that day (always a good start). Also, remember that reading is a useful way to join the conversation; spend some time getting used to the way people write and have conversations in Twitter.

Tweet – noun and verb: Let's be clear: a post on Twitter is known as 'a Tweet'. People also talk about Tweeting ('I Tweeted about X', 'She Tweets a lot these days').

@/At Reply: If you put the '@' symbol and the Twitter handle of another user, you are signifying that you are talking to them, publicly. Other people will see the @username as a link and be able to click on it to find out who they are and maybe what they have been saying that you were responding to.

DM/Direct Message: You can only direct message people who are following you. Be very careful when sending – use the Direct Message feature on the Twitter home page or the Direct Message feature on the tool you are using. Posting in the wrong way means everyone can see your message – potentially embarrassing.

Deleting messages: Speaking of embarrassing messages, you can delete Tweets if you get something wrong. Generally, it's best to do this straightaway if you can and put out a new Tweet with what you meant to say straightaway. If you have made a catastrophic error, it may be best to go back and delete a Tweet or Tweets. Whatever you do though, don't act as if no one saw them – deleting things may draw more attention to the issue, and others may well have seen the Tweets and recorded them elsewhere already.

RT/Re-Tweet: Along with the '@' messages, RT is another of the main abbreviations you will see in Twitter. It stands for 'Re-Tweet' and is someone re-posting someone else's Tweet that they have enjoyed or want to draw attention to. The RT is followed by the @username of the person with the original Tweet. Many tools will do this automatically for you, or you can cut and paste the original Tweet into your homepage.

URL shorteners: Because of the small amount of space you have to create your Tweet, Twitter users generally use URL shortening services, like Bit.ly, Tiny.cc and Snurl.com. Again, these are often part of Twitter tools (see below) but to use one on its own just go to one of the websites enter a URL and it will give you an alternative, short URL which will redirect anyone clicking on it to the original web page you wanted to share.

#/hashtags: Sometimes if people want to form a discussion pool of Tweets, they start adding a word with a pound-sign or hash '#' at the start of it. This means that other people wanting to see who else is talking about it and what they are saying can see it. During a big breaking news story or a sports event, you can often see what people close to the event are saying and feeling about things.

In Brighton in the UK where I live, for instance, there are two hashtags that I like to use: #Brighton, which gets Tweets picked up by the @Brightonfeed profile and gives you a seemingly random stream of Tweets about the city. Also good in Brighton is #bricom which gets picked up by the local paper's @brightoncommute feed, where commuters share information about (mostly) problems with the trains between London and Brighton.

(Note: If you're a Mac user, you can type '#' by pressing Alt+3. I just say so as it took me a while to work that out.)

Twitter search: Twitter suddenly starts to become even more useful when you use special search services. Twitter's own search engine is at http://search.twitter.com. Try using it to find mentions of things you are interested in or – once again – like hashtags to find all the posts about a news story or event happening at that moment.

Trending topics: Another feature which can really add to your experience of Twitter and help you explore its networks is 'Trending Topics'. You'll see this on the right hand side of the Twitter home page and search page, and many Twitter tools include a feature that lets you see them too. This picks out keywords and hashtags which lots of people are using. Clicking on one lets you see what everyone is saying about that subject. During big national or international sporting events, you will often see that event featured less there along with the names of leading sportspeople involved.

Twitter tools: There are thousands of services and tools that have been built to make Twitter easier to use. Many users now use a dedicated tool on their computer and/or phone to use Twitter. My personal preference at the moment is for Tweetdeck (http://tweetdeck.com/beta/), which is free and lets you set up a number of columns to see your Twitter stream – Tweets that are @-directed to you and Direct Messages – separately. It also carries columns for Trending Topics, Search, and you can use its

URL shortening and image upload features to post links easily. Tweetie (http://www.atebits.com/tweetie-mac/) and Seesmic (http://seesmic. com) are also popular for computers, while on the iPhone and other mobile devices there are a number of Twitter applications – some free and some costing a few pounds.

Photos and videos: To show people video and images via Twitter you can either link direct to them, use the built-in service in whichever Twitter tool you use or use services like TwitPic (http://twitpic.com) and Twiddeo (http://beta.twiddeo.com) to upload them.

Lists: You can create lists in Twitter of interesting people you follow or by subject matter. These will be listed on people's Twitter profiles and you can choose to follow their lists. If you create a list it will have its own web address. For instance, if I created a list of all the interesting people I follow in the education sector I could call the list 'Educators' and it would appear as http://www.twitter.com/amayfield/educators.

Building your Twitter use and presence

- Advice: There is plenty of it about, in the form of '10 ways to be a Twitter power user' and the like but make sure you approach it – as with all things on the web – with a critical eye. Refuse to accept that there is one, definitive way to use Twitter.

- Take your time: It's OK to take the time you need to learn how to use Twitter, and make it fit with your style.

- Growing your network: Have a look around your work-related networks and your local network to see if you can find interesting people to follow. Directories like Twellow, TwitDir and services like Twitterlocal.net will show you people Tweeting near to you. Many mobile phone and computer Twitter tools will show you who is Tweeting near you too.

- Regular posting: Find a style for posting that suits you. Some people have Twitter on in the background and dip in and out. My preference is to do one of two things: first, share the best things I find when I am reading online, when I am travelling or at an event. Second, I spend some time in a break or at the start and the beginning of the day looking at what others are saying and adding to their conversations or re-tweeting to pass on useful or interesting things to others in my network.

■ Be a loose connection: One of the most valuable roles to play in networks is connecting with different groups or people. Carrying news or interesting content from one to the other can prove very valuable to others. Aim to have a diverse set of feeds to follow: look for people in academic research if you are in business or vice versa, follow people in related fields and share their ideas across your networks. Taking knowledge from one place and applying it in another is the definition of innovation, and it can be very exciting to play a part in that.

■ Keep an eye on who mentions you: When people re-tweet what you have posted or talk about you by using @yourname, take a look at their profile and consider following them. It's likely you'll have something in common and they could turn out to be a good connection.

■ Listening: Be a good listener for as long as you like. Don't feel like you need to be bashing out Tweets for the sake of it. If you like posts and don't feel like you want to start Re-Tweeting yet, don't worry – maybe add them to your Favourites instead by clicking on the star icon next to the Tweet. It's paying them a compliment, but quietly, and will keep the Tweet bookmarked for you.

■ You don't need to read everything: Even after following just a few people on Twitter, it can start to feel like there is just too much coming through on your feed. Remember it is a stream of information and communication that you can dip into – if someone really wants you personally to see something they will send you an @message, a DM or use another way of getting in touch like email or text.

■ Flagging interesting things: Try posting a few links to things you have really liked – articles, images, videos, useful online tools – and see what reaction you get. Sooner or later someone will Re-Tweet something you have said and you'll realise that you are being listened to.

Playing the game

Like every other social network, people can approach Twitter as a game, a numbers game. How many followers can I get? How often can I get

Re-Tweeted? Like some video games, this can be fun for a while, and then it gets really repetitive. And it's not much fun for the other people in your network either (unless they are all playing the game too, I guess).

What you can end up with is a massive number of followers who become more of an audience than a network. You have no real relationship with them and it ceases to be a meaningful network – what Seth Godin calls a 'fake network'.

As with so many aspects of managing your web shadow, it is best to be yourself. That way you will not run the risk of triggering the 'crap detection' filters of people that you actually like and want to have a relationship with.

Alan Patrick, a consultant, dissected and ridiculed this echo-chamber mentality in a blog post entitled 10 Ways of Using the Twitter Egosystem (http://broadstuff.com/archives/1800-10-Ways-of-using-the-Twitter-Egosystem.html):

'the egosystem is that part of Twitter inhabited by those people whose sole purpose on Twitter is to "amplify" themselves. However, given that the poor things are so busy pimping themselves that it must be hard to think of all the ways and means they can do it, we have published this handy guide as a service...'

Further reading

While you wouldn't want to spend too much time reading about Twitter when you could be out there in the networks learning first hand, the following is a selection of blog posts and resources that I have found useful:

Getting started

Lifehacker: Practical guide to getting started on Twitter: http://www.lifehack.org/articles/communication/from-here-to-tweeternity-a-practical-guide-to-getting-started-on-twitter.html

Advice for one man bands and small businesses

Twitter's official guide for businesses on Twitter: http://business.twitter.com/twitter101/starting

Deep thinking

Laura Fitton's speech at Google on Twitter: http://video.google.com/ videosearch?client=safari&rls=en-us&q=laura%20fitton&oe=UTF-8&um=1&ie=UTF-8&sa=N&hl=en&tab=wv#

Desktop tools

Try one of these Twitter management tools for your computer:

■ Seesmic: http://seesmic.com/
■ Tweetdeck: http://tweetdeck.com/beta/
■ Hootsuite: http://hootsuite.com/dashboard
■ Tweetie (Mac only): http://www.atebits.com/tweetie-mac/

7. things you need to know about... blogging

'If you don't love something, don't write about it.'

Matt Cutts[65]

Why blog?

When it comes to the social web, blogging was my first love and it remains one of the most exciting and valuable parts of my working life. Establishing, developing and maintaining a blog requires significantly more effort and time than other elements of maintaining your web shadow, but the rewards are significant.

Blog is an abbreviation of 'web log'. It describes an online journal with (usually) the entries appearing in reverse order (the most recent appearing first). Other elements that are essential to a blog from my point of view are that you can subscribe to it (via RSS) and that readers can leave comments.

A quick note on terminology: blogging's still relatively new as a medium, even if it is one of the older forms of social media, so we will forgive our friends and colleagues if they get it wrong sometimes. But, for the record: a blog is the whole website, the journal, the place. A blog post is the unit, the item, the article that goes on the blog. You 'post on a blog' or 'put up a blog post'. When you write a post and publish you are not 'putting up a blog'.

Centre of your web shadow

A blog can give you a great deal of control over your web shadow, and potential to develop your personal online presence in all sorts of interesting ways. You can define its look and feel and pull together all the strands and streams of your different profiles and online activities in one place.

Search engines like blogs. In the language of the search engine optimiser's trade, blogs have fresh content (new posts regularly), are well

[65] http://searchengineland.com/googles-matt-cutts-video-presentation-on-seo-24234

connected (they link to lots of relevant, related, reputable pages and attract links similarly) and are 'crawlable' (the search engine can 'see' all of the content on the blog.

Because Google likes blogs, and if you connect your network of profiles (Twitter, LinkedIn, Flickr etc.) to it, it makes it all the more likely that you will appear high in search engine results for your own name. If you create a particularly useful blog professionally, it is likely that you will start appearing in Google searches for all sorts of keywords related to your field, helping people to find you.

Different ways people use them

'For mainstream journalism, with its newt-like attention span, blogging is yesterday's news. Twitter is currently the focus of media ridicule, but next month the circus will have moved on to something else... Mainstream media may have lost interest in blogging, but that just confirms the extent to which it has become an accepted part of life in the networked world.'

John Naughton, 'Everyone's invited to the birthday bash for Blogger', *The Observer* http://www.guardian.co.uk/technology/2009/sep/13/blogging-john-naughton-comment

- **Professionally:** Writing about your field is a good place to start. Make it a 'personal professional' blog, with appropriate disclaimers about not being the official views of your company. Check your company's policy on blogging and use of the social web – if they don't have one, drop a line to your boss or HR department letting them know what you are doing and, if necessary, assuring them you will steer clear of contentious issues.
- **Personal/general interest:** Some blogs are simply online, public diaries. If you decide to go down this route, do bear in mind that this is also your *de facto* professional profile. Employers, clients and colleagues are likely to come across it if they go looking for you online.
- **Activism:** Political and other causes are commons themes for bloggers. Blogs are a great way to spread information, rally supporters

and give momentum to causes. Once again, bear in mind that if this blog becomes a prominent part of your web shadow, it will in large part define your reputation online.

- **Public notebook/place to think:** Ostensibly, my blog is a professional one, concerned with the media, communications and the web. In theme, that defines it well, but I think of it as less of a personal publishing platform, and more of a public notebook, where I share ideas, develop trains of thought and share things I find interesting.
- **Team collaboration:** Blogs can work well for teams who want to share thoughts and files on a project. Sometimes it is appropriate to do this in public, or, if not, on a secure corporate network or password-protected blog (with a bit of due diligence around security issues). Blogging in private, or with a small team of people can be a great way for people to learn how to blog, and develop their styles before going public on the open web.

Getting set up
To host or not to host?

The first choice you have to make in setting up a blog is whether to have completely your own blog, or to create one on one of the blogging services. These are either free (Wordpress, Blogger) or will charge you an annual fee (Typepad).

I can't believe it's not blogging...

There are also some professional blog/online community services like Marcomprofessional (http://www.marcomprofessional.com/) for marketers that will host a blog, or take a feed from your personal blog elsewhere. Check if these are well optimised for Google by searching for the name of some members to see if they appear high in the search results for that name.

Another alternative to consider are services such as Posterous, which can act as a very straightforward blog that you can post to simply by emailing your content (a photo you've just taken on your phone, a link to a YouTube video you love) with a few sentences to a dedicated address.

Creating your blog

On hosted platforms: The process for creating your blog is pretty straightforward. There are likely to be 'how to' videos, and detailed instructions in the FAQ section of the site. Note that other than the URL (website address) and the name of your blog there's not a lot that you won't be able to change or tinker with later on until you get it more to your liking.

On your own server: Setting up a blog on a server is more technical than a hosted blog, but not impossible by any means for someone with only basic tech skills (I include myself in this).

I'd equate the complexity and effort in creating a blog with putting up a fairly large family tent for the first time. The instructions that come with those tents are hellishly dense, and often just in text form. But you feel your way through and get there eventually. Online of course we have the benefit of being able to ask our friends, our network or Google questions like 'how do I set up a blog on my own server'.

If at all possible, I would recommend co-opting someone who has done it before as it can help you through the tricky bits, but with some patience you can get there on your own.

Once again, check the Me and My Web Shadow website and also the Delicious section I mentioned before, where I will post as many helpful videos and resources for this as possible. However, these are the basic steps you will need to go through to create your blog:

Buy a domain name: You need to find a web address that no one else owns. With managing your web shadow as a starting point for creating this blog it will be good if you can buy your name, a variation of it or something in keeping with your web shadow (a play on your name, etc.). Most web hosting companies will sell you a domain as well and have tools to let you check what is available. Try to buy the '.com' or '.co.uk' suffixes for your address first of all, but failing that there are many more like '.eu', '.info' and '.me' that could also be options.

> Note: When you are filling out your domain registration and hosting details be sure to pay attention to WHOIS registration information. If you register with your home address and do not ask for this to be anonymous, people will be able to find it easily using WHOIS tools.

Find a hosting provider: There are lots of companies that will rent you a corner of a server, a computer that will give people access to your blog pages. There are a couple of considerations in choosing a package: storage (how much space you get) and bandwidth (how much people can download).

Choose an FTP client: Starting to sound pretty techie already, I know. File Transfer Protocol (FTP) clients (programs) let you move big files from your computer to a server and back easily. I use Filezilla (http://filezilla-project.org/), which is free and available for most computers.

Choose your blogging software: I am going to recommend just one piece of blogging software: Wordpress (http://wordpress.org/). It is by far the most commonly used blog software and with good reason. It is open source, which means that there is a vast community of volunteer developers working on it to make it better all the time, and a huge variety of themes (design templates) and plug-ins and widgets that let you do all sorts of interesting things with your blog. If you want to explore alternatives then some Google searches and trawls through the many blogs that write about blogging will give you the low down on options like Moveable Type and Drupal.

Naming your blog

Here are some routes you might take for creating a name for your blog:

- Your Name Here: You could, of course, just name your blog after yourself. Plenty do: Alfie's Blog, Byrne Baby Byrne and NoahBrier.com are three from the top of my reading pile.
- Sub-brand: Primed and ready to sound like a brand name that could even grow into its own company. Examples of this: BuzzMachine, Twopointouch and Puffbox.

■ **Enigmatic:** Creatively minded folk especially like to have an odd, quirky name for their blog. Casting a casual eye over feeds, I can spot them immediately: Crackunit, ::HorsePlgCow::, Feeding the Puppy and Usable Interfaces are four of my favourites.

■ **Literal:** A blog about my job. If there aren't many people talking about your field in blogs, this can be a very good move.

Whichever path you go down in naming your blog don't over-think the whole thing. Have fun with it, ultimately your blog, like a baby, will grow into the name and it will feel exactly right.

One more thing, although there are several million blogs in existence, it is best to be original with the name. Have a search for your title and make sure there aren't any others called exactly the same thing out there – it will just cause problems in the long run...

Design

Whether you host your blog yourself or opt for a hosted service, at some point you should take a look at dating the design. If you are using WordPress, there are literally thousands of free 'themes' that you can choose. With other platforms, the choice is more limited, but some tinkering with customisation options should give you something that is to your taste.

Anatomy of a blog

Think about who will visit your blog and what they will need

Everything about the way your blog is put together needs to be in the best interests of people who visit it. In web development circles this is called 'user centred design'. Basically, we need to constantly think about how this website can be most useful to the people who will visit it.

Reasons people are likely to visit include to:

■ read a blog post they have found a link for (in an email, in another blog post, through Google);
■ comment on a blog post they have read elsewhere (in their news reader, etc.);

- find out more about you or get in touch – they have been searching on Google for your name, or something to do with your business or area of expertise and have found your blog;
- get more of the good content you've been creating. Your blog post was great! What else have you got? Which other blogs are like this one?
- subscribe to your blog posts.

As I'm not a professional designer or techie, the easiest way for me to explain some of the choices and issues that will face you in creating and maintaining your blog is if I walk you through mine.

Have a look at my blog as an example. It is hosted on a server rented (from 5quidhost), lives on the domain www.antonymayfield.com and is called *Open (Minds, Finds, Conversations)*...

Design/theme

Consider these elements when thinking about the look and design of your blog:

- **Simple is best:** Black on white is easier for people to read. Complex designs may confuse or distract from content. If I had more time or money to invest in my blog I might have a better designed blog, but if I tinker too much or install a template that is beyond my technical knowledge to manage, I know the whole thing will just look like a mess (potentially a shiny, slightly pretty mess, but not much use to most visitors).
- **Columns:** This is a three column design, with the blog posts appearing on the left. Partly, I chose this because it is easier for people to see in a mobile phone browser – they see the text of the blog posts before all of the navigation and extras in the two other columns.
- **Space for badges and feeds:** Another reason to choose this layout was so that I could have badges and feeds or streams of content from other services like Flickr, Delicious and Twitter, which make the blog more interesting and also connects the different parts of my web shadow. My blog may pick up a reader from people viewing my Flickr

photos, and my Flickr photos may get more views because they
appear on my blog.

Description

Simple stuff, but a brief description of what your blog is about, and maybe
who you are. It will give visitors quick information about whether it will be
worth their while spending some more time here (are you interesting to
them?, are you the person they were looking for? etc.).

LinkedIn badge

This is a link to my profile on LinkedIn, which I have put high up on the
page so that people who want to know more about me can go straight
there, where they can also get in touch with me. The badge can also act
as a reminder to people who read the blog regularly that they might want
to connect with me on that network.

The help section in LinkedIn will give you instructions on how to do this.
Also, you can take a look at buttons, widgets, plug-ins and tools (the
same things get called different names in different places) that are offered
as standard with your blog – if these are on offer you should use them.

Photo stream

This widget brings a stream of the most recent public photographs from
my Flickr profile. It adds a bit of colour and personality to the blog – a
visual diary of things I have been doing recently. As I mentioned before, it
also connects the blog and Flickr profile parts of my web shadow nicely
too, showing visitors and search engines alike that antonymayfield on
Flickr and antonymayfield.com/blog are one and the same person.

Blogroll

Blogrolls are almost a venerable tradition in blogging terms. They list links
to blogs that you like, read a lot, or just plain recommend. They are helpful
to visitors as they show your network, and if they are interested in what
you are blogging about they will be able to find similarly minded souls in
this way. From a search engine point of view, these links are valuable as

they are permanently on your front page and on all the archive pages of your blog as it grows as well.

If you put someone's blog on your blog roll you are effectively paying them a compliment and giving them some 'Google juice', a bit of link reputation that will help them be more prominent in their networks.

Spam badge

The spam badge is automatically added by the Wordpress plug-in Akismet – it is advertising itself in return for the (free) service it does in blocking spam comments.

Bookmarks

Just like the Flickr stream, this section is bringing in my latest bookmarks from Delicious. It is a useful feature because it says 'if you like what I'm writing here, maybe you will find what I'm reading interesting'. And, once again, it is connecting two important parts of my web shadow: my Delicious and my blog.

Twitter stream

With the Twitter stream, my latest Tweets appear on my blog as well. It is a useful prompt for people who enjoy the blog posts to take a look at what I am up to on Twitter and maybe connect with me there too.

Recent comments

The 'recent comments' section is a really important feature for me in a blog. It shows people where debate is happening on the blog, which may not necessarily be on the most recent post. This feature helps bring comments, the life of the blog as a social space, to the fore.

Blog post
Headlines

If you want to be found by people searching on a particular subject you need to use a plain, everyday language description of the topic. The closer it is to the words people will put into a search engine looking for information on this subject the more likely you are to appear in the results with a link to your post. I thought I was being a bit oblique when I wrote 'Learning to read Twitter' as the headline of this post, but actually it is a very literal explanation of what I am talking about.

That said, don't over-think this aspect of it, the most important thing is to get on with writing interesting posts as often as you can. Sometimes I will go down the route of punning, playful headlines on my blog posts, but that is because I think of the blog as much more of a public notebook than a serious publishing play. Write because you're interested in the subject rather than because you are desperate to gain attention for your blog.

Images

Using images in blog posts is a good idea. It brightens them up both on the page and in the news reader where most people will see them. Use photos as illustrations or literal illustrations. Make sure you have a good screen-grab utility for grabbing shots of websites or pictures.

Be aware of the rights of the people who own images. You can search for Creative Commons-licensed images (see the videos about Creative Commons at http://creativecommons.org/videos/ for an explanation of how this alternative to copyright works) on Google Image Search, Flickr and other services. Make sure you credit people where necessary and link to them in your post or directly from the photo (the image settings on your blog editor should let you do this).

Hyperlinked text

Blogging is a direct descendant of Tim Berners-Lee's original proposal in every way. Make sure that when editing your blog post you link wherever it is useful, especially:

- **Definitions:** If you use a word that is jargon, a new concept, or that may need further explanation link to somewhere that explains it.
- **Articles you are referencing:** Link to the source if you quote someone or talk about a post or article.

■ **People and organisations:** Link to someone's home page, blog, LinkedIn profile or, if they are notable enough, to their Wikipedia entry.

> **Note:** Wikipedia is one of the best places to link to for many things. Often it will explain a company or product more clearly than the official web pages.

Writing with links is a skill in itself, and you will develop your own style as you do it more and more. It helps with the short form of blogging (you don't need to provide context or explain yourself as much), and makes your posts a part of a broader theme or topic on the web rather than standalone little bits of text.

Quotes

The convention in blogging is to indent text which is a quote. This makes it easier to identify as a quote from elsewhere. As so much blogging is building on or commenting on content from elsewhere it is important to follow this style (and link to your source) – your blog editing interface or software will usually do this for you automatically when you highlight text and press the quotation button.

Embedding video and other content

Videos on the web, and things like slideshows and documents from SlideShare and Scribd can be made part of your blog post by embedding some code in it. Don't worry, though it sounds technical, once you have done it once it is really simple. On a YouTube video, for instance, you will see a box to the right of the video with the word 'embed' next to it.

Highlight the text and copy it.

Then in your blog editor, change your view to HTML and you will see any words for your post that you have written already and some characters that are 'code' – notes for the blogging platform about fonts and paragraphs etc. Paste the video into the text where you want it (after a

<p> means you are pasting the video after the paragraph break at the end of a sentence). Then switch back to 'visual' or normal view.

> **Note:** Check the FAQs and advice in your blogging platform for more advice. Also, blog editors like Windows Live Writer for PCs (free) and Blogo for Macs (at a cost) will have ways of doing this quickly and simply.

Sharing options

At the end of the post are some prompts to share the post. You can choose what options to give people in the settings for your blog or with plug-ins, depending on the platform you are using. I have opted to prompt people to share on Twitter and also provided a 'Share This' button, a service which will give someone access to buttons for sharing on many different social media platforms and email.

Categories and tags

To be honest, I don't use categories. If you set them up for your blog, keep them simple or you will create a headache for yourself and your users as over time they become more sprawling and complex.

Tags are keywords, as in Delicious, that describe the post. The beauty of tags is that they are helpful for finding posts on a similar subject, but they don't tie you in to the onerous task of managing a taxonomy of categories.

Over time, they can provide you and users with a useful way of seeing what you have been writing about. I display a 'tag cloud' on the front of my blog, in which the tags I have used most often make up the largest words. Visitors can click on these to see all of the posts on that topic.

Comments

Comments are precious things on a blog. They show it is alive and that people are reading it and are interested enough to comment. Every comment is a compliment, attention being paid to your posts, even when they are disagreeing with you.

A word on moderation: You can usually adjust the settings on your blog allowing you to either approve comments before they are shown or just allow them to appear straightaway. My preference is for the latter, since I don't want to get in the way of a discussion just because I'm busy and not able to see and approve comments as they arrive in email. That said, many people pre-approve comments after having had trouble with 'trolls' (persistent online troublemakers). See what works for you.

Lastly, your blog is *your* house and people who visit need to respect your rules. If you feel someone is being offensive feel free to delete the comment, but be sure that that you aren't just in disagreement with their point of view. (See Part II's *Dealing with bad things online*.)

Blogging workflow

Even taking a low-level approach, blogging can take a lot of time. One way to deal with this is to think about the different elements involved and tackle different tasks, different parts of the workflow at different times of the day. Sitting down in front of a blank screen and demanding a blog post from yourself can work for some, but for most of us we need to tackle blogging in a bit more of a structured way.

Reading

It is hard to be a good blogger without being a good reader too. You will need a newsreader and Twitter network (*see Useful tools for managing your web shadow* and *Things you need to know about… Twitter* chapters in this section) to do this really well. Find a couple of places where you can stash interesting ideas for blog posts.

Personally, I have a folder on my desktop where I save notes with links to things I want to write about. Additionally, if you use Delicious or another online bookmarking tool, they can often provide a set of things you can share with others in a blog post. Google Reader's 'star' function's great if you want to read posts on your mobile phone while travelling or in spare moments and mark ones that might make for an interesting topic to post about.

One tip: If you find a post that you think is interesting and want to blog about it, go and read it on the original website. As well as amends or updates, you are likely to find some comments which add to the piece and that will lead you to other interesting bloggers and posts about the same topic.

Writing

There are of course, as many ways to write a blog as there bloggers, i.e. millions. These are my guidelines and advice, but bear in mind that for each one there will be an exception and that, as you master the art of blogging, you may decide to be an exception to one, many or all of them.

- **Little and often:** Blog posts work best as a short-form, partly because of where they will be read (computer screens, laptops, mobile phones). Blogs come alive most when there are regular posts. Conversations start and feature in the reading lists of a regular crowd, so try writing lots of short posts, especially at first.
- **Be interesting (to yourself):** Just get on with talking about things you find interesting. If you worry too much about an imagined audience chances are you will be wasting energy and getting it wrong most of the time. As professional blogger and journalist, Felix Salmon puts it: 'you have much less of an idea what your readers are going to like than you possibly imagine'[66].
- **Ask open questions:** You don't have to be right or have all the answers on a subject just because you are writing about it on a blog. In fact, it can be liberating to admit that up front, and pose your emerging points of view as questions. 'Can it really be this way? Is there a case for the industry/movement/wider society to do this differently?'
- **Don't worry about perfection:** As Slate's Farhad Manjoo says, 'don't worry if your posts suck a little'. You have to learn by doing when it comes to blogs. The first time I pressed 'publish' on a blog post, my heart was in my mouth, adrenalin surged through me. What if everyone hated it? How long before a throng of bloggers I admired

---

[66] Slate: How to Blog: Advice from Arianna Huffington, Om Malik, and more of the Web's best pundits: **http://www.slate.com/id/2207061/**

turned up to take apart my futile efforts. But you get used to it quickly and learn that it is more important to get posts out there, get thoughts aired and get the conversation going, than to have each post unassailably right and polished.

■ **Make blogging a treat, not a chore:** Once you have mastered the basics, blogging can become a great pleasure. The space and time it gives you for stopping and thinking about what is happening in a field you are interested in is invaluable.

Editing and publishing

Treat editing your post as a separate activity. Once you have finished writing your finely tuned post, shake your head clear and re-read it to make sure it makes sense. Correct any obvious typos and grammar errors and add in your links.

Often, writing a blog post brings your thoughts together in new ways and new ideas emerge as you are writing. As a result, I regularly find that the most interesting paragraph has been written at the end. If this happens, think about bringing that bit of text further up in the post or copy it and paste it in italics at the start by way of a teaser or introduction to the post.

Promoting and connecting your blog

If you are particularly pleased with a blog post or think it could create some debate, don't be shy about letting people know. Put a link to it on Twitter, post it on your Facebook and LinkedIn status updates and let people know in brief what it is about. If you have some contacts and colleagues who you know will be interested, let them know and ask them if they would comment if they feel moved to do so.

It's best not to push your blog every time there is something new on it as people may find it a little annoying after a short while.

Naturally, it is also a good idea to connect your blog to any other profiles you have on social media and social networks. As the natural centre of your web shadow, you should make sure it is linked to/mentioned wherever you are. For instance, my company routinely refers to personal/professional blogs of its employees when they are mentioned in press releases.

Directories and search engines

Establish an account with Technorati (http://technorati.com/), a specialist search engine for blogs, and link it to your blog. You may also find blogger directories that you can register with to ensure that anyone using them can find you. I wouldn't say that either of these things are priorities, but they are part of making sure your blog doesn't miss out on opportunities to get noticed.

Analytics

Blogs' analytics are the measurement tools that record what happens to your blog – when visitors are arriving, where they are coming from, and what they are looking at.

Looking at the data around your blog is surprisingly easy, interesting and useful in itself. It can teach you all sorts of things very quickly about how the web works and how your blog is performing. It can also be mildly addictive to see how many hits or links you are getting from other blogs and websites, which, especially while you are learning your way around blogging and trying to develop a routine, is no bad thing.

There are two sets of data you should take an interest in initially: your blog's analytics and Feedburner's analytics.

Blog analytics

Most hosted blog platforms will give you access to basic data about who is visiting your blog and which posts they are looking at. Often you will be able to install plug-ins that will give you more in-depth recordings of data about visitors. I use both Google Analytics and Statcounter, which are both free (although you can pay more for advanced features in Statcounter).

Have a play with whichever analytics software you have access to, but some interesting questions to start off with are:

■ What articles are popular? You may find an off-the-cuff short post is getting vastly more attention than your heartfelt diatribe setting the world to rights. It's worth asking why and digging into the links and search terms that have sent traffic to a popular post.

- What keywords in search engines are including your blog posts in the results? At first, you are likely to see your blog posts appear in search engine results on niche topics and terms, or via specialist blog search engines like Google Blog Search.
- Where are people coming to your blog from? Analytics data can tell you a lot about the people who visit your blog. Often digging into the information about an individual (just follow the links) can tell you what company they are from and which part of the world they are in.

Feedburner

Most of the attention for blog doesn't happen on the blog itself. More people read it via RSS feeds (in their email, news readers or on personal aggregators like iGoogle and Netvibes). The Feedburner service from Google will – with a little techie tinkering – let you run the feeds from your blog through and then get data on how many people are subscribing to your blog and how many are reading posts and clicking through to your blog from feeds.

Advertising

It is relatively easy to have some adverts on your blog, but it is unlikely to make you very much money at all unless you have a significant audience and are treating your blog as a serious publishing venture. If you are using a free hosted service, you will most likely have ads served on your blog (Google, for instance, gives bloggers a share of revenue from ads on their Blogger platform).

If you are interested in learning more about, for instance, how Google's AdWords system (which provides keyword ads on websites), the Google Search engine and other Google services like Gmail work, then it could be a useful exercise in the same way that you can learn a lot about search engines and links from looking at your analytics. Otherwise, investing time in getting ads to appear on your blog may not bring much of a return and, if handled clumsily, may make visitors' experiences less rewarding.

Further reading

- iCrossing: How to start blogging – free ebook at http://bit.ly/icblog
- Andrew Sullivan, 'Why I blog', *The Atlantic*, November 2008 at http://www.theatlantic.com/doc/200811/andrew-sullivan-why-i-blog
- *Blogging for Dummies*. Hoboten:Wiley Publishing Inc, 2008
- Socialtext: Media Literacy Wiki: Blogging: https://www.socialtext.net/medialiteracy/index.cgi?blogging
- Lifehack: Blogging for Newbies: http://www.lifehack.org/articles/communication/the-newbie-guide-to-blogging.html
- Slate: How to Blog: Advice from Arianna Huffington, Om Malik, and more of the Web's best pundits: http://www.slate.com/id/2207061/

conclusion: connected lives and serendipity engines

This book leads with the idea of your web shadow as being about reputation. And reputation, what you say about yourself, what you do and what others say about you, is an important reason to take note of your digital footprint, your web shadow.

As you will have realised there is, of course, more to it than that however.

While there are risks and dangers for us as our lives become enmeshed with and empowered by the web, there are enormous opportunities that far outweigh them.

To care for your web shadow is to be present in the web, to be a connected person. There are so many benefits to being connected, for yourself and for society at large, and they are so varied and so personal it would be foolish to try and categorise and define them here.

The big reason, the meta-reason as a geeky sort might say, to be connected is to be lucky, or at least luckier.

One phrase which kept rolling around my head while I was writing was 'serendipity engine'. The more I have used the web, the more open I have been, the more I have shared the more happy coincidences that have occurred for me.

I searched and found a couple of posts and articles about this idea already – itself a kind of serendipity[67]. Then Joshua-Michéle Ross on the O'Reilly Radar blog posted the first of three interviews with John Hagel, a management thinker I have a lot of respect for[68].

Hagel was discussing why the the importance of networks, of being in them and using things like Twitter to connect and communicate with

---

[67] Shane Richmond's Telegraph.co.uk blog post 'The Web is the Best Serendipity Doo Dah Ever Invented' is a particularly good read: **http://bit.ly/S6Tta**

[68] O'Reilly Radar: John Hagel on the Social Web, by Joshua-Michéle Ross: **http://bit.ly/1dEK6F**

people, is that it increases your chance of finding the right person with the right knowledge at just the right moment. The most valuable knowledge, Hagel argues, is not lying around on intranets and the web, waiting to be found by a search engine. It is inside people's heads, and can be unlocked by context and connections, by a happy coincidence, or the right question asked of the right person at the right time!

Being a part of the web, the social web, the growing network of people, improves all of our chances of being lucky. In aggregate it could make our communities, our organisations, our countries, the whole world luckier when it comes to finding the right answers at the right time.

In a world where we face so many challenges, I see hope in the web, in the idea of connecting all of our minds, and ideas and knowledge.

You take your first step to understanding this by exploring how the web connects to you. Maybe by putting your name into a search engine or a social network and finding out what is there. Then why it is there. Then how you can change that.

Then how you can change the world.

I really hope that this book has been useful to you. Let me know what you think and come have a look at some of things I've found out about since at www.antonymayfield.com/webshadows.

Antony Mayfield
Redroaster, Brighton, November 2009

index